Finding the Time

THE SPIRIT OF SIMPLE LIVING

Finding the Time

SHARON HANBY-ROBIE

Guideposts®
CARMEL, NEW YORK 10512

Acknowledgments

Every attempt has been made to credit the sources of copyrighted material used in this book. If any such acknowledgment has been inadvertently omitted or miscredited, receipt of such information would be appreciated.

All material that originally appeared in *Daily Guideposts* is reprinted with permission.

Scripture quotations marked (AMP) are taken from *The Amplified Bible*, © 1965 by Zondervan Publishing House. All rights reserved.

Scripture quotations marked (KJV) are taken from *The King James Version of the Bible*.

Scripture quotations marked (NIV) are taken from *The Holy Bible, New International Version*. Copyright © 1973, 1978, 1984 International Bible Society. Used by permission of Zondervan Bible Publishers.

Scripture quotations marked (NKJV) are taken from *The Holy Bible, New King James Version*. Copyright © 1997, 1990, 1985, 1983 by Thomas Nelson, Inc.

Scripture quotations marked (NLT) are taken from the *Holy Bible, New Living Translation*, copyright © 1996. Used by permission of Tyndale House Publishers, Inc., Wheaton, Illinois 60189. All rights reserved.

Scripture quotations marked (TLB) are taken from *The Living Bible*. Copyright © 1971 by Tyndale House Publishers, Wheaton, IL 60187. All rights reserved.

www.guidepostsbooks.com
1-800-431-2344
Guideposts Books & Inspirational Media Division
Developmental Editors: Cristine Bolley and Deb Strubel
Cover design by Wendy Bass
Interior design by Cindy LaBreacht
Photo by Stockbyte Platinum/Getty Images
Typeset by Nancy Tardi
Printed in the United States of America

Contents

Introduction

Time plays such a major part in how we live our lives. Sometimes, it seems that time is as slow and sweet as a gently rolling river. And other times, it nearly knocks the wind out of us—more like the roaring white water of a stormed river. The busier our lives get, the less time we seem to have. And when we are waiting for something, the time of anticipation can seem to last forever. Time will run us ragged unless we find balance and learn to use it to improve the quality of our lives.

Obviously, we can't control time—it is going to run its course. The sun will rise and set every day, as usual, no matter what is going on in our lives. Everyone has the same amount of time—the key is to use it well. What makes the difference is how we view time as it relates to our lives at each particular moment.

It's important to step back and gain some perspective on the fact that you only have one life to live. Are you satisfied with how you are spending your time, or is there room for a little improvement? Are you living your life with purpose and doing what you want to, what God wants you to do, or is someone else pulling the strings?

First accept reality; time is limited. No matter what happens in your life, a day will still only have twenty-four hours, a week only seven days, a year only fifty-two weeks. But also accept your limitations. It has been said that youth and youthful energy is wasted on the young, which means the older you get the longer it takes to accomplish what you must. As the phrase says, "Don't major in the minors." Learn to make the main things the main things.

In this book, I will present ways to balance time, making it work *for* you rather than against you, so that the gift of time will help you achieve your heart's desires. And I hope you will experience a glimpse of God's perspective of time and His plan for your life. After all, His view is the most important one of all.

—*Sharon Hanby-Robie*

Finding the Time

PART ONE

Facing the Reality of Time

TIME IS NOT A RESPECTER OF PERSONS: It doesn't spoil one person by giving him or her more of it while depriving another by giving less of it. On the contrary, time is the great equalizer. We all are given the same amount of time each day, to use however we decide. To feel satisfied with the days of our lives, we must learn to use time honestly. So to truly enjoy the way we use our time, we must learn to simplify our to-do list, appropriate time for what is important and leave some "wiggle room" for God's surprises each day.

Enjoying the Moment

"So don't worry about having enough food or drink
or clothing. Why be like the pagans who are so deeply
concerned about these things? Your heavenly Father
already knows all your needs, and he will give you all you
need from day to day if you live for him. . . . So don't worry
about tomorrow, for tomorrow will bring its own worries.
Today's trouble is enough for today."

—MATTHEW 6:31–34 (NLT)

How many times have you said, "There just aren't enough hours in the day"? Even if I don't say it, I certainly think it almost every day. My to-do list is endless, and I never seem to get everything done that I think I should. I long for a moment to myself, where I can pamper myself or simply soak in a hot tub. When I become overwhelmed, I want to run away! And occasionally, I do run away to the beach.

I am always amazed at how simple life can really be at the waterfront. I recently spent a week at the Outer Banks of North Carolina. It was my first trip there. It wasn't exactly what I expected. It's far more developed than I thought it would be. There is a lot of traffic and tourists. Nonetheless, my spirit still seemed able to slow down as I heard the rhythm of the ocean.

Despite the fact that this was a working vacation, I was still able to leave behind the daily stress, work and frustration, and enjoy the time I spent there. As the Lord instructed us in Matthew 6, I didn't worry about tomorrow and I didn't fret about the day before—I simply lived one day at a time. I woke early each morning and took an hour-long walk on the beach. The sand felt so good under my feet. I loved watching the pelicans dive into the ocean hunting for their breakfast. I laughed at the sand pipers as they danced from each oncoming wave. I *relaxed* in the beauty of God's artwork. That fact simply amazed me.

How is it that life can seem so simple at the beach—away from home? And why do I need to drive eight hours to experience something that seems so fundamental to my well-being?

Perhaps we simply live in a world gone mad—living in the fastest paced society ever. As Americans, we work more, we work faster and we take fewer vacations than most of the world's labor force. Is it that we *are* restless, or is it that our quick pace makes us *feel* restless? I am always anxious to finish whatever I am doing as quickly as possible (except for my vacation). But it makes me wonder, why do I feel compelled to work so hastily? It might make sense if I were hurrying to get work done so I could "enjoy" a few moments. But usually I am only planning to move on to the next task and repeat this hectic process all over again. So what's the point?

SIMPLY PAUSE FOR A MOMENT

Inside, a voice is saying, *Enjoy the moment.* Can you hear it? I know it's hard to hear with all the chaos going on around you, but if you listen carefully—you will hear the whisper of your Maker.

Unfortunately, without us even being aware of it, we are often so preoccupied with the running list of what we are going to do, or what we were supposed to do yesterday, that we don't hear His whisper. We miss the present moment when He speaks. What makes this so significant is the fact that the only moment over which we have any control is the one we are experiencing right now! Unless we learn to be aware of this very moment in time, we will eventually find that we have missed some of the best moments of our lives.

Guideposts writer Van Varner asked what I think is a very poignant question when he wrote:

> If you were given a gift of time—let us say a twenty-four-hour day—what would you do with it?
>
> I ask this because as I write this we are in a leap year, and the calendar has thrown in a joker, a day in February that hasn't appeared for four years. What a boon! What an invitation to do something unusual! But what?
>
> "Quite seriously," said my friend Mary Lou, "if I were given the opportunity to do anything I wanted, I'd spend it in solitude."
>
> "I'd spend it outdoors," said Mary Ruth. "I'd try to find the perfect place to wander in nature, to get as close as possible to God and His creation."

"Frankly," said my buddy Harold, "I think the thing should be declared a worldwide, quadrennial holiday. Close the banks, open the pleasure palaces, let's all go to the beach!"

As you can see, it takes all kinds. And that includes those who said they'd go on a museum binge or "clean out my attic at last," or those who told me that they'd look for some unusual way to help others.

So I suppose you're wondering what I would do with this unexpected gratuity. Actually, I made my choice weeks ago: I'd treat February 29 as though it were a day like any other. Why? Because of something I remember my old boss and mentor having written years ago. "Today has never happened before," Norman Vincent Peale said. "It's a glorious opportunity to start all over again."

That's it. A glorious chance to change my attitude, to wipe the slate clean of grudges and grime. That's the real gift I'm being given, time to start over. And I can do that today and tomorrow and tomorrow. . . .[1]

The fact of the matter is that you always have enough time to enjoy this moment or any other moment—it's simply a matter of choice. Only you have the power to decide whether or not you will enjoy this moment. Like Van Varner said above, today is a good day to start all over again and make the choice to enjoy today!

SIMPLICITY MADE SIMPLE

Here are some ideas and a few exercises to help you get your new start:

You can actually teach yourself to **ENJOY THE PRESENT**. Learn to concentrate on breathing. Slowly take in a deep breath. Then focus on learning to feel your breath fill your lungs and expand into your stomach. As you slowly release it, you will feel yourself slowing down. Repeat this exercise five times.

To enjoy the moments of your life you must learn to live life with more aware-ness. For example, by **TAKING A LEISURELY WALK IN A BEAUTIFUL SETTING** you can teach yourself to be more aware of the present moment. Be sure to keep your pace consistent—don't rush—as this is to be a break from your nor-mal routine. Pay attention to your movements and relax as you take in the beauty of your surroundings. Once you have mastered this technique in a beautiful place, you can adapt it to wherever you are—work, play or home. You will soon be discovering things about your surroundings that you never noticed before.

If like most of us you are doing more now than ever before and accomplish-ing less, well, it's time for a change of pace. Start by making a wish list to **IDENTIFY GOALS** that you want to accomplish. Then allow yourself the free-dom of time to put a plan into action. That way you will actually spend your allotment of time on the things you want to do instead of just being busy.

Remember these wise words of Henry David Thoreau, "Why should we live with such hurry and waste of life?"[2] We must **LEARN TO LIVE MINDFULLY AWARE**, and that requires living at a slower pace. Unless we slow down we will never have time to reflect on our lives. Without reflection we won't even know what we are running from or to. Take a few minutes at the end of each day to reflect on all that happened. Define the single most important moment of the day. Was it good? Or was it not so good? Regardless, learn from that moment.

Live as if your life depended on it, because it does. Unless you take the time to **PAY ATTENTION TO YOUR BODY, MIND AND SPIRIT**, you will not hear them when they cry for attention. Make a conscious effort each day to connect with all your parts. If you have a pain in the neck—then take a moment to massage it out. If you experienced a particularly wonderful moment this day—then take another moment to write it down in a journal. By the end of the year, you could have a whole book of wonderful moments recorded.

Take advantage of the liberation in Christ's words (Matthew 6) and live your life in the freedom of today. Begin to **SEE YOUR LIFE AS AN INSTRUMENT OF GOD**. His will, not yours—moment by moment. When you do, life can only get better.

> **Lord, I trust You to take care of all my needs, including food, clothing and shelter. Because You have told me not to be anxious, I will embrace today without anxiety. I will live each moment fully aware of Your goodness in my life.**

Simplifying Time

Better one handful with tranquillity than two handfuls
with toil and chasing after the wind.

—ECCLESIASTES 4:6 (NIV)

Remember the phrase, "The hurrier I go, the behinder I get?" It's the modern equivalent of the above verse. When we are constantly hurrying to accomplish as much as possible, we cannot successfully give anything our best effort. As we rush haphazardly through life, we get careless, frazzled, and lose touch with what's most important. We are foolish when we become workaholics driven either by greed, envy or the desire to stay ahead.

As Solomon tells us in Ecclesiastes 4:6, busy lives will only bring stress and problems. Unless we learn to live in moderation, we will miss out on the blessings and rewards God wishes to bestow on us for work well done. Hurrying through our work is certainly not going to allow us to do a good job. Tasks may get done—but at what cost? God wants us to enjoy His gifts and realize that He is the One in charge of handing out the daily work assignments—not us.

Filling our schedules with too many good things is not necessarily a good thing. We all must learn to say no. Although this is a hard lesson, it is a necessary one. Unless we learn to say no even to some good things, we will never have enough time for the important moments.

Time is perfectly democratic and equal for all. As author and speaker Og Mandino says, "You possess as much of this precious commodity as the richest person in the world and yet you may not realize how wealthy you are."[3] He continues this thought further with English novelist and playwright Arnold Bennett's statement, "No one can take it [time] from you. It is unstealable. And no one receives either more or less than you receive."[4] If this is true, how is it that some people seem to have time on their hands while the rest of us are racing to beat the clock and running like chickens without their heads?

The key is learning to cherish the time we have and make wise choices about how we can best use our time. We must first figure out where we are currently spending our time and then choose to spend it on only those things that are really important. Ultimately, finding more time is about simplifying our lives.

IT MAY BE TIME TO LET GO OF SOMETHING

My friend Elaine has always agreed to take an exchange student for the summer because she believes this is an important ministry. By having an exchange student in her home, she and her family are able to demonstrate God's love to someone who otherwise might never be exposed to His mercy any other way. She also believes it is a great lesson for her children to learn about and better understand other cultures. Nonetheless, it creates stress and discipline challenges in her home that require more of her time to deal with than would be necessary if it were just her own children at home. Finally, after much prayer and angst, she decided not to take in a student this year. And what a difference that made in her life and the lives of the entire family. It was a difficult decision, but she made the right choice. It gave her and the family more time together—which is important because her children are now teenagers and will soon be leaving the nest. This was a wonderful gift of time that will have long-lasting impact.

Making better use of time is a learned skill that we all can acquire. When we finally do learn this lesson, it will seem like we have *more* time. The truth is that time doesn't change, but we can. We can't buy or barter for more of it. The only way we can affect it is to eliminate something from our to-do list.

When I was younger, I thought I really could have it all. But now I realize I can't. Although time seems like it is moving faster than ever, it is relative to how I choose to live my life. Time doesn't stand still; it doesn't run faster, it remains the same. But there will always be enough of it to do the things that are important—if we make the right choices.

As we learn to de-stress our lives by simplifying our schedules and making better choices for the use of our time, we will find an abundance of time for family, friendships and staying healthy. When we refuse to make time our prison, we can instead use it to set us free. As Winston Churchill once said, "Men stumble over the truth from time to time, but most pick themselves up and hurry off as if nothing happened."[5] Wouldn't it be a shame if you missed the truth that God has for your life, simply because you rushed right past it? As Fulton Oursler, Jr., former editor-in-chief of *Guideposts* magazine, wrote:

Jesus, Whose grace was given us before time began, spoke of the last days when earth's time will stop. And in the few seconds it took to write that sentence, I have had thoughts that span the entire arc of time. For an instant, the great puzzle seems clear. Everything—from the first nanosecond of time, through what we call the past, the present and all that is to come—happens at a pace no clock can measure. It happens in God's good time.[6]

The next time you consider taking on another pet, hosting another family dinner, or organizing another charity event—stop and consider the value of the precious time you have been given. Then consider the risk of taking that allotment away from those you love most. Is it worth it? As Benjamin Franklin said, "Dost thou love life? Then do not squander time, for that is the stuff life is made of."

In the end, it's not about how much you get done—but the quality of what you do. Time really isn't money—it's your life. Learn to make the most of it.

SIMPLICITY MADE SIMPLE

Here are some thoughts that may help you simplify time:

It's clear you can't buy more time, but you may be able to *share* your time and accomplish more. For example, **ARRANGE A TIME-SAVING EXCHANGE WITH A FRIEND**. If you are going to run errands—give her a call and see if she has errands that you can do for her as well. Then, the next time she does her own list, hand her your list too! That way you each save a little time for more important things—like sharing a cup of tea together.

Take a good look at your life and how you currently spend your time. What things are you doing simply because you always have? Are they necessary? Are they things that enrich your life or merely add to your work and stress? Recognize that **YOU MAY NEED TO GIVE CERTAIN THINGS UP**—even if only for a season. When I was going through a difficult phase in my life, I realized that what once brought pleasure and fulfillment was now only adding to my stress. I finally had to give up my position as the music coordinator for our women's Bible study. I had loved that job, but during that particular time in my life it simply was too much of a good thing.

Sometimes the easiest way to de-stress is to **AVOID RUNNING ERRANDS AT RUSH HOUR**. I used to think that it made sense to run my errands while I was returning from an appointment. Then I realized that if it turned out to be rush hour—running my errands took twice as long! Now, instead, I run my errands at off-peak hours.

SCHEDULE DOCTOR APPOINTMENTS AT OFF-PEAK HOURS. Ask the scheduling nurse or receptionist what time is the least busy for their office and arrange your appointment then.

In order to use wisely the time you have been given, you will need to invest a little of that time in planning and organizing it. Careful planning for regularly scheduled and out-of-the-ordinary events is one of the simplest ways to find more of this precious commodity. Although it may seem like a mundane and boring task to **USE A CALENDAR OR PLANNER**, in the end you will be glad you did it.

Avoid the guilt of breaking a commitment you never should have made in the first place. It is easy to allow the stress of the moment to coerce you into saying yes when you should have said no. Whenever you are asked to take on a new task or role, **GIVE YOURSELF SOME BREATHING ROOM BEFORE MAKING A DECISION.** Simply say that you will need a little time to think about it. Then decide if it really fits in your schedule without the pressure of having to answer immediately.

PRACTICE SAYING NO. For many of us, saying no is difficult. We feel guilty and uneasy. One way to make this easier is to prepare in advance by practicing how we will say no. That way, when someone surprises you with a possible commitment, you will be prepared and feel at ease enough to say no. First of all, always be honest. A statement such as "I really have a lot on my plate right now, so I better not take on any more" is straightforward and shows that you know how to prioritize. There is no need for you to further explain or justify your answer. You are simply making the most of the time God has given you.

FIND TIME TO QUIET YOUR SOUL. We all need time with our precious, heavenly Father. Only He can refill us when we feel drained. It is when we give ourselves the time for solitude with Him that we will find God's provision and clarity for our everyday lives.

> Lord, I choose to say no to the busy habits that I have practiced, and yes to taking time to be with You today. It is better to enjoy quiet moments with You than to strive for something that You never asked me to do.

Time for Family and Friends

Redeeming the time, because the days are evil.

—EPHESIANS 5:16 (KJV)

The above verse seems difficult to understand at first. The *New Living Translation* says, "Make the most of every opportunity for doing good in these evil days" (Ephesians 5:16).

Once you study this verse, it becomes clear that its lesson is a very important one. When Paul says these days are difficult, he is communicating his sense of urgency at evil's pervasiveness in our lives. We all need to recognize this sense of urgency because our days are difficult too.

Our lives are filled with an overabundance of work and excessive responsibilities that make it a struggle to succeed at it all. As Christians, we know that we should keep our standards high, act wisely and do the best we can. Yet, in the midst of all our duties it is easy for our good judgment to fall prey to the demands of life. Without our even being aware, we can end up neglecting the ones we love.

We all value our time with family. We believe and intend for our families to be our top priority, right after God. We know that the proper order for our lives is God, spouse, children and church. Yet, without any bad intent, spouses often get pushed to the back of the line.

Many women who juggle the chores of raising a family, caring for a home, and often a full-time job outside of the home, are simply drained with no time or energy left at the end of the day. As a result, husbands get neglected. Yes, they are adults, they should understand. And they do try to . . . but eventually, continued neglect can lead to building a wall of separation that can be difficult to remove. The longer the pattern of neglect continues, the deeper the separation. Spouses living indifferent and busy lives can lose touch, intimacy and eventually their interdependency.

Most of us want our primary relationships to be the best they can be. A spouse should be the first recipient of our time. A healthy relationship requires that we give our best to it. Yet, if we honestly step back and count the amount of time we actually put into our relationship with our spouse, we may be saddened at the lack of quality time spent.

IT'S TOGETHER TIME

If you are married, when was the last time you had a real conversation with your spouse, while looking into each other's eyes? If we want our mates to feel important and treat us with the same importance, we have to start making them a significant priority. That means setting time aside just for the two of you—alone. No kids, no business, no phone calls, just the simplicity of time together.

Men also fall prey to the same kind of action. They get busy at work. To keep up they start coming home later and later each evening. When they get home, they are distracted and unable to change focus. This makes it difficult for them to interact with the family.

Recently, my hubby and I have been attempting to give each other five meaningful contacts a day. You would not believe how hard that is! In the morning, he will kiss me on the cheek and say, "That's one!" At the end of the day, I often am still waiting for number two. And we're really making an effort! That's sad. How can it be that hard to simply make contact a few times a day? The simple answer is that we are letting our lives get too busy. But at least we are now aware of it. We have communicated the fact that we both need more time together. It's a start.

Parenting is a full-time job. Yet lack of time has taken its toll here too. Did you know that most fathers only spend a few minutes each day interacting with their children? Of course, the catchall excuse is, "We may not spend a lot of time together, but when we do it's *quality* time." Try convincing a five-year-old of that. A child is only a child once. And that time goes very quickly. Just take a look at the past year's videos and you will see how much has changed since you last looked. We cannot make up time with our children or grandchildren because they will soon be adults. And then it will be too late because they will be busy too.

Guideposts writer Dolphus Weary wrote about his own awakening experience regarding time spent with his children:

> For years, my family and I have taken vacation trips. Well, at least to me they were vacations. We have been to Chicago, Montana, California and many other places, including our home state of Mississippi.

We had great times, I thought, and that is why I was so shocked when last year on our vacation in Oregon, my three children came to me and said, "Thanks Dad. This is the best vacation we've ever had!"

"We've been on so many trips before. What do you mean?" I asked.

Danita answered, "Dad, you gave us your attention. You didn't call the office every hour worrying about what was happening there."

Reggie stepped in and said, "Yeah, and you weren't dragging us from house to house, staying with people we didn't know."

I could see out of the corner of my eye that even though my wife Rosie didn't say anything, she was agreeing with them.

I thought about what they said. It was true, I wasn't turning every moment into a public relations meeting to raise funds for our ministry. Instead, I was spending time with the children and my wife . . . as a real vacation should be.

I had to sit back, take a deep breath and know that I was hearing truth from the lips of my children. I wanted to say, "Don't you remember when . . ." but the words "Thank you for being open and honest with me" came forth. "I am glad you are my children."[7]

Dolphus was lucky he got the message in time to make a difference. As we learn to be more aware of how we choose to spend our time, the quality of all of our relationships will improve.

SIMPLICITY MADE SIMPLE

Here are some thoughts to help you find more time for love and family:

As you search for more time to spend with family, **BE AWARE OF THE ACTIVITIES THAT YOU CAN FORGO.** For example, rather than spending hours each week growing the perfect vegetable or spending too much time shopping, try purchasing your veggies at the local farm market and do some of your shopping online, until life affords you extra time.

FAMILY RITUALS are a great way to stay connected. Whether it's reading your children a bedtime story, or spending twenty minutes each night as a family catching up on the day's events. And don't forget to pray together—it is the best remedy for what ails today's families.

MAKE TIME FOR COMMUNICATION. When communication breaks down between couples, everything about their relationship suffers. Think about the areas of life that are most important to you as a couple: parenting styles, family occasions and other demands. Even though these can be areas of discourse between couples, they often never get discussed. Together, decide how you will handle them. Once you are aware of the issues and have taken the time to discuss them, you will be prepared to deal with them when they happen.

DON'T FORGET TO PLAY. Spontaneous fun can be some of the most pleasurable times. But planning for fun guarantees it will happen. Laughing is good for the soul! My goddaughter regularly reminds me that she needs laughter. So I am always ready with a joke or two to get her back on track.

It's the little things that count. **FIND THE TIME TO WRITE LITTLE NOTES OR CARDS**, and hide them in a place where you know they will be found. Unexpected mementos are nice too. Do this both for your children and your spouse. The other day I bought my husband a small box of candy—for no reason. He's still confused as to why I did it—but he's enjoying it! You gotta keep 'em guessing.

Life is better with a few good friends. All healthy relationships also need a break. **CULTIVATE A MEANINGFUL RELATIONSHIP** with someone of the same gender, same value system and same age. My friend Jan and I have been fortunate to be able to share life together for eighteen years. We walk together, talk together and pray together. This time shared has kept us connected, on track and healthier both physically and spiritually. We make sure that our calendars are never too full for each other.

CHERISH YOUR FAMILY DINNERTIME. *Parade* magazine ran an article about games that get parents and kids talking. It wasn't a surprise to me that one of the most effective ways to get your kids talking is to have dinner together. Dinnertime for our family was "family" time. It was loud, full of laughter, tears, and lots of support. The author of the article, Bruce Feiler, said his family also used this time to reconnect. But their family had a couple of rules for each evening: "Don't greet your father with bad news at the door. Let him open the mail, change and decompress before being walloped with news of cavities and bad grades. Next, my parents would retreat to a behind-closed-doors hour where they would dispense with their own news—bad and good. That left dinnertime for talking with us."[8] I think that those rules make a lot of sense for today.

Father, help me to walk wisely and take every
opportunity I can to do good and encourage those
I love by giving them the attention of my time.
Thank You for always having time for me.

SMILE—God Loves You!

And the peace of God, which passeth
all understanding, shall keep your
hearts and minds through Christ Jesus.

—PHILIPPIANS 4:7 (KJV)

Remember the television show, *Candid Camera*? I loved watching it. People are just so amazing; it takes so little to get them riled up. The program simply placed people in situations that any one of us could find ourselves in. Then we all watched as human nature took over. And boy did it ever take over! Then . . . just when the person was about to lose it . . . the producer made that now memorable announcement, "Smile, you're on *Candid Camera*!"

What's even more amazing is that every day, every one of us is being watched by God's "candid camera." He sees and hears everything we do. If we stopped and thought about that more often, we would probably be less likely to let our human nature have so much control over situations. It's not so much that we scream and yell at others; it's more about how we grumble, fret and worry, or stew in anger over something someone did or didn't do. As a friend of mine told me years ago, "If worry would put one penny more in my pocket—I would do it. But it can't—so I won't." And we all know that anger hurts the person holding the grudge more than the person to whom it is directed. Life is short enough—why waste this precious time on something so unproductive?

Scripture tells us that God guarantees us His peace. His peace will not necessarily remove all conflict from our lives or even put us in a permanently positive state of mind. If we really know God and have an intimate relationship with Him, then we can rest and not worry or fret because we see He is in control and *that* is perfect peace. But instead of trusting God with our lives, we set ourselves up for disappointments by our own expectation of what life should be like.

We allow ourselves to be anxious over the possibility of what *might* happen or, worse yet, we become disappointed by expecting others to be something they are not. I remember years ago having a conversation with my brother about our father; my brother kept expecting my father to be more than he really was. The problem wasn't our father—it was my brother's expectations for him that caused the conflict.

Every time our father didn't meet my brother's expectations, my brother was hurt and let down. Yet, he brought it on himself—Dad never made any promises to be different or better. But my brother had this image that he thought Dad should live up to. Instead of achieving a peaceful relationship with our father, my brother created a situation that brought frustration, anger and pain. When my brother finally accepted the reality of who Dad was, their relationship improved. What's sad is all the time he wasted in pain that could have been joy.

FILL YOUR TIME WITH POSITIVE EXPECTATIONS

When we focus on the positives instead of the negatives in our lives, our lives improve. All of us have frustrations, problems, physical ailments and a history of things we could consider bad in our lives. So why is it that some people seem to be happy and enjoying life and others don't? The difference is attitude. When we adopt an attitude of joy through God's peace, life is better—despite the bad and ugly things in it.

People with a joyful attitude expect good things from life, and they usually find them. People with a negative attitude experience more negative things because that's what they are looking for.

Guideposts writer Daniel Schantz experienced God's peace in a unique way:

> I was feeling bitter toward God about a project that fell through. As I finished breakfast I muttered my complaints under my breath. "It would have been so easy for You to make it work out, God," I complained. "It really makes me mad." As I headed for the car, I felt like a hurt little kid as I slammed the door behind me.
>
> All day long I was nervous, as though I expected God to strike me down for being so angry with Him. Instead, I had one of the happiest days of my life. Later, when I told my wife Sharon about it, she smiled and said, "Just because you were angry with God doesn't mean He is angry with you. After all, God is kind, even to His enemies."
>
> "But I was furious . . ."
>
> "Maybe so," she replied. "But all relationships are like that. You and I get upset with each other, but it doesn't mean

that we really hate each other or want to hurt each other. It's just part of communication."

"But God is different," I insisted. "I didn't have any right to be angry at Him."

"Oh, I don't know. I think if I were God I'd be flattered to think that you felt close enough to trust me with your strongest feelings," Sharon concluded.

Later that evening I read the apostle Paul's instructions: "If you are angry, don't sin by nursing your grudge. Don't let the sun go down with you still angry—get over it quickly" (Ephesians 4:26, TLB). And that reminded me of the poet William Blake's words:

> I was angry with my friend:
> I told my wrath, my wrath did end.
> I was angry with my foe:
> I told it not, my wrath did grow.

Now I see that by telling God just how angry I was, I was being truthful. I also could let go of my anger, instead of nursing it. God doesn't quit loving me just because I'm mad at Him, or turn off the gifts of His wonderful grace. He calls me His dear child. (Ephesians 5:1).[9]

How beautiful life can be when we walk first with our Creator. He knows best, He cares best, and He plans to make the most of our time here on earth if we just let Him. No matter your mood or your situation—put on a smile— I guarantee things will improve.

SIMPLICITY MADE SIMPLE

Here are some other ideas to help your life get a little brighter:

Pastor Robert Schuller called it the "tyranny of unpleasant memories" when we allow unpleasant memories or old hurts and disappointments to haunt us.[10] When we surrender to these negative thoughts, we give them control over our future. Instead of living for our dreams, we are imprisoned in regret. Make a choice today to **SET YOURSELF FREE FROM NEGATIVE THOUGHTS**.

Life is uncertain—and that is not necessarily a bad thing! Instead of focusing on all the *bad* things that *might* happen, **LEARN TO BE OPEN TO ALL THE GOOD THINGS** that *can* happen.

Norman Vincent Peale said, "If it's important how we begin each day, so is it equally important how we end the day. Begin it right, live it right, end it right—and you will have a good day every day." Take time at the end of every day to let go of the day's worries and relax. Count the happy moments and then **END YOUR DAY WITH READING GOD'S WORD**.

TALK BACK TO YOURSELF! Listen for that negative thought and when it comes, simply replace it with a positive one. The quickest way to shake out a negative thought is to talk back *out loud*.

We all have moments of frustration and anger—and that's okay. Just as Daniel Schantz learned when he expressed his honest feelings to God, the key is not to stay angry or frustrated. Allow yourself only a short period of time to experience the negative or frustrating thought. The amount of time should be relative to the situation. When the predetermined time period is up, **MOVE ON BY LETTING GO** of the negative thoughts. It's time to move on to happy thoughts!

The world is filled with God's astonishing wonders! **REDISCOVER HOW TO "WONDER."** The ability to have thoughts of wonder is part of God's creative design. Some call it being visionary; others say it's learning to capture our dreams. No matter the name, it's all about learning to consider the positive possibilities. Awaken the dreams that God has planned for you by allowing yourself some time to dream with the gift of wonder!

SMILE AND THE WHOLE WORLD SMILES WITH YOU. When I first moved to Pennsylvania from New York, people thought I was pretty weird. I talked funny, I dressed funny, and I smiled. I smiled at people as I walked down the street—I even said hello. Evidently, this was not something that normal people around here did. But now, twenty-three years later, a lot more of us weird people have moved here. Guess what has happened. More people are smiling. Hmm . . . just imagine the difference you could make if you smiled at everyone you encountered today? Try it, it works!

> Lord, I am amazed when I consider the wonders
> You have created. I am filled with peace knowing
> that nothing is too hard for You to turn around
> for my good. Thank You for keeping my feet
> from stumbling as I follow You.

Important vs. Urgent

If the ax is dull and its edge unsharpened,

more strength is needed but skill will bring success.

—ECCLESIASTES 10:10 (NIV)

Former President Dwight D. Eisenhower said, "The urgent problems are seldom the important ones." Yet we easily get caught up in the urgent issues and never get to the ones that really matter. Most of us have good intentions, but success depends on implementation. With only so many hours in a day, we render ourselves ineffective when we waste precious time doing the things that are not truly important.

There are problems every day that scream for our attention, so much so that we feel compelled to deal with them when the fact of the matter is there were far more important things we should have done instead. For example, we know we should start working on organizing our important financial papers. But day after day, we spend time answering e-mails that could have waited or returning phone calls that don't really need to be done today. Before we know it, half the day has passed and it's too late to tackle a project as large as organizing our paperwork.

The problem was that the paperwork didn't ring like a telephone demanding that we answer, nor did it send us the "you've got mail" message. So it was easy to ignore it. That doesn't change its importance; it simply means it was quietly waiting for us to decide it was time to tackle the project.

Prioritizing the level of importance for a task is a skill—a skill we can all learn, but a skill nonetheless. As the verse from Ecclesiastes shows us, trying to do anything without the necessary skills is like chopping wood with a dull axe.

DON'T MAJOR IN THE MINORS

If we want to do a better job of prioritizing the important things in our lives, then we need to recognize where the problems are and acquire honing skills. Most of the experts use a four-category method for determining which items are important and which are urgent. Stephen Covey, in his book *The Seven Habits of Highly Successful People*, used a four-quadrant method to depict levels of importance.[11] *Urgent* matters, Covey explained, are visible, immediate and often gratifying to tackle. But *important* matters, because they may seem less pressing than the urgent ones, are often postponed. To achieve success you must attend to both types of matters.

The key to effective time management is identifying both urgent and important matters and deferring those items that aren't urgent and important. By creating a list in priority order you can simply define where you should spend most of your time. Here's an example that I use:

1. **Urgent and important:** These are the activities that are both urgent and important, such as deadlines, crises and other "do it now or else" tasks. Often these are things that I need to attend to on a daily basis. I call this my "crisis management" list. These are things that I find to be draining or stressful. As an interior designer, these urgent and important tasks include the calls I receive from clients with problems. Yesterday, a client called and the sofa that was supposed to have three pillows had only two. This is a crisis for her. No matter what else I was doing, I had to drop it and deal with this issue. It's an issue that is important to both of us and it was urgent because she was upset. But it forced me to give up something else that I had planned on doing during that time.

2. **Important:** These activities are important but often ignored because they're not urgent. Covey refers to them as the "soft," people-centered activities that enhance our lives and our relationships. Things like "building relationships, writing a personal mission statement, long-range planning, exercising, preventive maintenance, and preparations—all those things we know we need to do, but somehow seldom get around to doing."[12] This is where our spiritual life should be listed.

3. **Urgent:** These activities usually call for immediate attention but are *unimportant*. They are very high priority, second only to the crises issues that we first listed. They are

phone calls, meetings, e-mail, chores, and the never-ending interruptions that fill most of our days. Their level of priority or urgency is usually established by other people, which puts us in a reactive situation rather than one over which we have a lot of control. The sad thing is that we can end up spending a lot of time doing them. For me, this is the paperwork that most jobs or employers require. It doesn't accomplish much. It doesn't change whether I do a good job or not. It simply gives someone a record of what I have already done. And it takes me away from doing what I should be doing instead of preparing reports. (Can you tell I dislike paperwork? I do—and I admit it!)

4. **Luxury:** These are things we should only do if we really have the luxury of extra time, which means these are things that are not important at all. Unfortunately, we often spend time doing them to avoid doing what's really important. These are basically time wasters. Covey says, "People who spend their time doing these things basically lead irresponsible lives. Effective people stay out of [numbers 3 and 4] because, urgent or not, they aren't important."[13]

At the end of the day our allotment of time is up—no matter what. Unless you chose to make the majors (important things) a major part of your day, you will soon find yourself living only with the minors (the unimportant events and things)—and that can be a very frustrating place.

SIMPLICITY MADE SIMPLE

Here are some tips to help you accomplish the most important things first:

Hal Urban, a leader in the Character Education movement, says, "Of all the positive ways to invest your time, this is number one. If you'll set aside ten minutes each day (the night before or first thing in the morning), **WRITE DOWN THE THINGS YOU WANT TO ACCOMPLISH,** number them in order of importance and keep your list visible throughout the day, you'll be amazed at how much more effective and productive you become."[14] Try it—unless you do, you will never get to the things you feel are most important.

ACCEPT YOUR LIMITATIONS. As we get older, our minds may be more ambitious than our bodies. Be realistic about what you can accomplish in a day or you will defeat yourself before you even get started. When I was young, I could be dressed and ready to see clients in a half hour. Now, if I want to look good, it takes the better part of an hour!

LEAVE A LITTLE WIGGLE ROOM in your schedule. I always plan for the unexpected "urgent" interruptions by making sure I have a few extra open days in my schedule to compensate.

Determine **WHAT ONE THING WOULD HAVE A POSITIVE EFFECT** on your personal and professional life, if you did it on a regular basis. For most of us, it is the important things that fall into Category 2. This is the foundation for our lives: our spiritual walk, our relationships, and our personal maintenance and growth. Without a strong foundation, the walls of our lives will crumble.

SET DEADLINES. This is especially true if you are a procrastinator. Just last night my husband and I were talking about his habit of procrastination. For the last month, he has postponed putting his closet back together after the new carpeting was installed. As we sat chatting, he told me how frustrated he was with himself because he simply couldn't seem to get this together. I asked him to try to set a reasonable deadline for himself and then work at it a little at a time. He responded, "Okay, how about two months?" "You've already wasted one month," I replied. "So you now have exactly one month left!" We'll see what happens. It's hard to change old habits, but at least he is aware and has verbalized it. That's a start.

Remember that the important tasks require you to **BE PROACTIVE**. Unless you take the initiative to get them started, they will never send you an e-mail or call you on the phone to remind you that they need doing. Only you can decide how important they are by the attention you give them.

SPEND EIGHTY PERCENT of your time working on the important things. The rest of the list only merits twenty percent of your time.

Rather than tackling the easiest things every morning, **START WITH THE MOST IMPORTANT**. Often the most important tasks can be the hardest, which is exactly why we avoid them. But your energy level will be higher to see it through to completion than if you attempt it when you are already worn out.

Remember the wise words of Dr. Denis Waitley, founding director of the National Council on Self-Esteem: "Of all the wisdom I have gained, the most important is the knowledge that **TIME AND HEALTH ARE TWO PRECIOUS ASSETS** that we rarely recognize or appreciate until they have been depleted. As with health, time is the raw material of life. You can use it wisely, waste it or even kill it."[15] The choice is yours.

Lord, I put my hope in You, for You give me strength
and cause me to succeed. Direct my steps so that
I use my time today to accomplish what is important.
Hold back the distractions that are sent to
tempt me from the way I should go, and bless me
with skills I need to fulfill Your purposes.

PART TWO

Using Time Well

TO LIVE WELL we sometimes need to ignore our watches and simply dwell in the presence of time, being content to know the day instead of the hour. To have more time to enjoy life, we also need to recognize what may be stealing valuable moments from us that, once mastered, will put balance back into our schedules. In this section we will observe the rhythm of life's activities so that we can use the momentum that comes with well-planned moments. We will also evaluate the real price of multitasking and discover that taking time to savor each moment may result in the greater use of time we are given each day.

The Daily Log

Now this is what the Lord Almighty says:
"Give careful thought to your ways. You have planted
much, but have harvested little. You eat, but never
have enough. You drink, but never have your fill.
You put on clothes, but are not warm. You earn wages,
only to put them in a purse with holes in it."

—HAGGAI 1:5–6 (NIV)

S ometimes I feel like I have worked as hard as I can but have still missed accomplishing something important. Or I get so busy that I start leaving things half undone. Like the other day, I had only two small loads of laundry that needed washing. Although it was already 7:00 P.M., I thought, *I can easily get these finished before bed.* Then the phone rang, then I started dinner, and . . . the next morning I discovered that I never closed the lid on the washing machine, so the first load never even washed!

This is unusual behavior for me—I consider myself overly organized and too on top of my game to be this absentminded. Okay—I am getting older—but I was surprised at myself. What if this had been something more important? *"Give careful thought to your ways."* The message from Haggai was registering loud and clear with me.

At some point, we all have to take a careful look at the pattern of our lives. With the busyness of our jobs, homes, children and other activities, it is too easy to fall into a routine rut and stay there. At the end of the day, it is easy to forget where we have been or what we have done. Our days begin to run together. We live by the clock. We cram our schedules so full that we hardly have time to think about whether or not we even want to do the things we are doing.

TO FIND TIME YOU MUST LOSE IT

In the last chapter we spoke about the four big divisions of activities that help us determine what is urgent and what is important. This chapter is about the daily routine of our lives. This is about our daily to-do lists and how the clock plays a role in our lives.

My husband has no clock in his world. It took me a long time to figure this out. If I ask him to do something, and he agrees, then I must accept the fact that he intends to do it sometime . . . which could be today, or tomorrow, or next month . . . but it *may* mean he intends to do it sometime before he dies. We were recently discussing this issue again when he said, "I think I now have a morning clock, but I still don't have one for the evening." I can tell you that he does not have a clock that runs for the entire week, month or year. I guess I should be grateful that at least he now *has* a clock—even if it only works in the mornings.

Ultimately, I think the best way to live is to find the balance between living by the schedule of the clock and my husband's way of not even having a clock.

Guideposts writer Eric Fellman wrote this interesting story about his own experience with his watch:

> I had to pack lightly for my trip to Africa. We used light planes, four-wheel-drive utility vehicles, and foot travel for short distances. I was pretty proud that my baggage consisted only of a backpack and small shoulder bag. However, I soon discovered that not all baggage is external.
>
> One day we were visiting a rural village and had an appointment scheduled that evening in a distant city. Like many of the people of the world, most Africans are not slaves to their schedules, so I was constantly checking my watch and reminding our African friend and guide of the need to speed things up. Aware that my haste would keep me from really getting to know the people we were meeting, he stopped at one point and asked to see my watch.
>
> Holding my left wrist with his right hand, he stretched his bare left wrist out next to my watch and said, "It is a very nice watch. We have a saying in Africa: All Americans have nice watches, and yet they never have any time, while few Africans can afford a watch, yet we have all the time we need for each other."
>
> I got the point, and soon afterward took off my watch and buried it in my backpack for a few days. Of course, I dug it out again the night we left for home, so we wouldn't miss the plane. But I've found myself going without my watch from time to time since then. Try it sometime. You'll be amazed at how much time frees up when you leave your watch at home.[16]

Like Eric, so many of us spend our time on things that keep us busy rather than on what is important. Time-management experts recommend keeping a daily log of how you spend your day in order to learn how to better live it. One expert suggests logging your activities every fifteen minutes. (I think that person is a crazy control freak!)

But if we never seem to have time to do what needs to be done, I do think we need to log our time—at least three times a day—with a summary of what we have spent our time doing. That, combined with a daily to-do list, will help us learn to create more time for the things we really want to do.

I am a list person, meaning I always write down what needs to get done. For me it's not about age—I have always used lists to keep me from forgetting important things. A written list helps me focus and allows me the freedom to think creatively instead of constantly trying to remember my commitments.

Unless we learn to give proper time and placement to what matters most, we will be like the people of Haggai's time who planted much but harvested little. Our own temples (spiritual life) will be in shambles while we fritter away our time on running errands. But if we give careful thought to our ways, we will work less and accomplish more.

SIMPLICITY MADE SIMPLE

Here are some thoughts to keep you running on time:

KEEP A DAILY TIME LOG for the next week. Then evaluate your time and how you have spent it. How is your time divided across work, business, family, spirituality, recreation and health? What percent of time did you spend on "important" items from our previous chapter? How much time did you spend with the people who are important to you? How much time did procrastinating waste?

What kind of **ADJUSTMENTS** can you make to the above time inventory? Are there any activities that you can eliminate from your schedule? Is there something that you can delegate?

One of the most beneficial aspects of keeping a time log is the realization that many things take much longer than we anticipated. By getting a **MORE REALISTIC IDEA OF TIME** you will learn to budget your time better. This will go a long way in reducing your stress.

If you would like to **TRY A MORE COMPREHENSIVE TIME LOG**, which is especially helpful if you have a full-time job, here is one way to do it: Make a list with the following divisions: Time, Activities Scheduled, Interruptions and Urgent. As you go about your daily activities update your time log every ten to twenty minutes, or every time you switch activities. As you add entries to your "time" and "activities" portion, be sure to note whether you were interrupted or if it was an urgent task. By keeping a log of this nature, it will be easy to spot time wasters and make changes that will help you become more efficient at your job.

KEEP A TO-DO LIST. (I like to use the long, narrow-lined paper pads.) Keep your to-do list in a place where you can easily add to it and mark off the things you have completed. First thing in the morning and before you go to bed, review your list and update it. Treat it like a game—the more you cross off your list, the higher your score!

Simplicity authors Barbara DeGrote-Sorensen and David Allen Sorensen pose an interesting question, "If you had a bizarre disease that allowed you to be conscious for just one hour a day, and knew your physical needs would be taken care of while you were unconscious, how would you use that one hour each day?"[17] This is an excellent question that enables you to easily **PRIORITIZE YOUR LIFE**. The point to the question is that those things you choose to do in that one hour are the things that probably mean the most to you.

Good time-management skills give you more control of your time and your life, which will reduce your stress level and increase your energy level. As you make progress you will be better able to **MAINTAIN BALANCE** between your work, personal and family life. In addition, as you learn to use your time wisely, you will find flexibility in your schedule that will allow you to respond to new opportunities such as playtime with your children or grandchildren.

Dear Lord, as I carefully consider my ways, I see that
I need Your help in planning my time. Help me to
recognize what is important, and guide me so that I will
be fully satisfied at the end of my days.

Time-Stealers

Thou shalt not steal.

—EXODUS 20:15 (KJV)

A thief is someone who takes the property of another. Most thieves use the advantage of surprise to steal. They sneak up quietly and suddenly take off with our precious belongings. Years ago, my home was robbed three times in two years. It reached a point where I was so angry that if I had encountered the thief, I would have attempted to capture him myself! Just like that thief in the night, people or events rob us of our precious time.

As I continued my research on finding ways to better use our time on a daily basis, I was surprised to find that there are, in fact, two different kinds of time-stealers. But as I will explain more fully later, they are related in an unanticipated way. The two different classifications for time-stealers are *external* thieves and *internal* thieves.

External thieves are things that most of us consider outside our control such as: unexpected or prolonged phone calls; a traffic accident; maintenance issues;

machine trouble (cars, washing machines or ovens); interruptions by children, co-workers or others; required business lunches or dinners; or an incompetent cashier at the grocery store.

Internal thieves of time include such things as: not delegating what we should; resisting change; acting scattered; not setting deadlines; tolerating disorder on our desk or in our home or closet; trying to be perfect (and not accepting anything less); not planning or setting priorities; indecisiveness; inability to say no; or simply avoiding responsibility.

There is an interesting relationship between these two thieves of our time. If you look carefully at both lists, and are honest with yourself, you will find that the external thieves are simply more internal thieves disguised in other trappings! For example, you may argue, "A traffic jam—how could I have known about that? Surely, that's not my problem, or anything that I had any control over." But the reality is that if you *plan* for the unexpected, a delay in traffic wouldn't have such a negative impact on your schedule.

ANTICIPATE AND RESCHEDULE INTERRUPTIONS

My drive to where I often work is one hour, and that is if there are no traffic- or weather-related problems. As a result, I always allow myself an hour and a half to get to work. That way, I can be reasonably assured that I will arrive on time. If I don't encounter any problems, I have time to relax and have a cup of tea. The same is true of the unexpected or prolonged phone call. You, and only you, have the ability and the authority to simply say, "This is not a good time for me to continue this conversation. Let me call you back later."

How about a washing machine or oven malfunction? The answer is the same; if we perform regular maintenance on all our machines, cars, etc., we will decrease the number of unexpected malfunction incidents. Obviously, we cannot plan for every contingency and real emergencies do occur occasionally. But the reality is that we have more control of the things that steal our time than we are willing to admit. The good news is that we do have some control and that means we can begin to eliminate some of the thieves from stealing our time. But first we must recognize that not everyone will be similarly motivated to accomplish this task.

Some people are happy living with the time-stealers because these unexpected interruptions fill a void in their lives. For example, people who frantically run around at the last minute looking for their shoes or their keys before dashing off to catch a plane probably enjoy the excitement and attention that this event brings to them. Still others use their time-stealers as manipulative tools. An example of this is the chronically late person who may enjoy the authority they feel subconsciously by preventing the others from proceeding. And those who take on more work than they know they can handle may do it just to make themselves feel important.

We are complicated beings who often don't know our own minds. As a result, we can too often sabotage ourselves and not even know it. That is why going through the process of reevaluation and honestly exploring what we do is so important to our future maturity, growth and success.

The truth about time is that although we cannot change it, add to it, slow it down or speed it up, we can change how we respond to it and thereby better control the time we have. The mastery of your time is a skill. Just like any other skill, it will take time and practice to learn and perfect it. The biggest obstacle to mastering time is in not knowing ourselves.

Unless we know ourselves well enough, and are willing to be brutally honest about our shortcomings and motivations for allowing time-stealers to affect us, we will fail. Most experts will agree that what makes this skill more difficult is often our inexperience at knowing how long something will take or how much time we really have available to accomplish it. It is only by taking a close look at what we actually do each day, and measuring the time each event takes, that we will be able to make precise and informed choices.

Whether we are cleaning our homes, or brushing up on our Shakespeare, it is critical that we know how much time is required in order to successfully do the job correctly. Like the adage says, "If you don't have time to do it right the first time, when will you find time to do it again?" Time is one of the most precious commodities in the world, yet it seems so easy to waste it. Until you learn to deal with the time-stealers, you will be robbing yourself of precious life.

S I M P L I C I T Y   M A D E   S I M P L E

Here are some tips on how to keep time rather than waste it:

Always try to plan ahead. A well-planned life is a stress-free life. **DON'T LEAVE IMPORTANT THINGS TO CHANCE.** For example, if your car is due for inspection or oil change in October, make the appointment for late September or early October. Not only will you have an easier time making an appointment that is convenient for your schedule, but you will also avoid the chance of driving with an expired inspection sticker or ruining your engine.

LEAVE EARLY ENOUGH for meetings so that you have time to spare.

BE SELECTIVE in how you use the time you have. Think twice before turning on the television for the evening. Television watching is addictive—before you know it the half-hour news program that you planned to watch has consumed an entire evening.

MANAGE NECESSARY TIME-STEALERS. I try to fit all my daily reading into one hour before dinner. I try hard to read or at least skim all publications that I've received that day. For example, I read the newspaper and skim professional journals and magazines on a daily basis. I mark or tear out any article that I want to read in its entirety. Then I place it in a pile to read later in the week.

CREATE ORDER. We all function better in an atmosphere that has a sense of order with flexibility. Suppose you have established that Monday is your day to do laundry and your washing machine breaks down. You want to complete the task to maintain order and stay on schedule. So you may decide to go to the Laundromat while the repair is being made. This demonstrates flexibility regarding the specific location—but maintains order in your schedule.

Plan to be organized. Rather than just browsing through the store and hoping something catches your eye, **MAKE A SHOPPING LIST AND STICK TO IT**. This will cut down on the time it takes to shop for groceries, clothes and gifts.

STOP PROCRASTINATING AND AVOIDING YOUR TO-DO LIST. If you catch yourself procrastinating, ask yourself why you are doing it. Knowing why is the first step in finding a solution. Perhaps you fear failure, so when you procrastinate the immediate pressure to complete the job is relieved. This may feel good, but it is temporary. Eventually, the guilt about not doing the job will take over, and then the pressure from the people counting on you will begin to mount. In the end you have simply made the situation more stressful than it was to begin with.

Some of the **TOP TIME-STEALERS** are watching television, Internet perusal, reading e-mails, reading the newspaper, talking on the phone and playing video games. These are not necessarily bad things; they are simply things that we may have trouble walking away from. Take control and make a choice about when and how much time you want to spend on these activities. Then stick to your time-specific limit.

PRACTICE MAKES PERFECT. In the end, only you can make a difference in what you do with your day. Remember to monitor your progress, and be sure to keep those time-stealers from robbing you of your life! You have a family, friends, and God all out there waiting to spend some time with you.

> Lord, Your Word says that wisdom will multiply my days and add years to my life, and that if I lack wisdom I can ask You for more.[18] Please give me wisdom, so that I do not procrastinate or waste my time today.

Streamline Your Time

Those who obey him will not be punished. Those who are
wise will find a time and a way to do what is right.

—ECCLESIASTES 8:5 (NLT)

This verse, in the *New Living Translation,* says that those who obey will not be punished. Those who are wise will find a time and a way to do what is right. Wisdom makes good use of time. Time is what it is, but if we use the wisdom of good judgment and apply proper procedures to our use of time, we can learn to accomplish more in the time we have. And I think that sounds like a very "wise heart."

In a time not so long ago, life seemed to move a bit slower. As a result, most of us had time for transition before we moved from one task to another. Today, with new technology and daily pressures, we are usually forced to move immediately from one task to the next without any time for our brains to reflect on what was good about our finished work, or plan how to better approach the new task before us.

If our brains were like our computers, we could simply click from one program to the next and we would be on our way. But God didn't design us that way.

Our brains are amazing wonders, but unlike computers, our brains respond emotionally as well as technically. We operate more like a symphony in perfect rhythm—not like a computer program. We need time between tasks to process whether what we did was effective, and then change gears for the next action.

Yet our fast-paced society forces us to ignore our natural rhythm, thus robbing us of the rest and reflection for which we were designed. We are supposed to take time to make good choices, to wisely adapt to new circumstances and collect our thoughts. Instead, we are attempting to move forward at a pace that can only lead to mistakes and inefficiencies in our daily lives.

If we learn to better coordinate the sequence of our activities, we will find more room for creating the rhythm we so desperately need to easily accomplish them. The goal is to improve the quality of how we use our time without detracting from the effectiveness of it. That is best accomplished by actually engaging our brain in the process. Those who are most successful at this task will gain the benefit of a more pleasurable experience.

FIND THE RHYTHM

One way to make better use of our time is to learn the art of streamlining. Streamlining can be applied to repetitive or similar activities and to activities that we are not particularly good at or don't especially enjoy doing. Two of the simplest ways to streamline are (1) learn to schedule together duties and chores that go well together, and (2) learn to delegate.

Let's start by focusing on the rhythms of our activities. For example, I wouldn't recommend trying to redecorate as you clean a room from bottom to top. Decorating requires a creative process that doesn't flow well with the rhythm of cleaning. My friend Cris couldn't figure out why it took her a day and a half to clean her house when her housekeeper could clean all four bedrooms, three living rooms, two dining rooms, a kitchen, and three and a half bathrooms in just a few hours. So one day, she carefully observed the procedures that her housekeeper used. What Cris realized was that her housekeeper kept moving, but when Cris cleaned she would stop to reorganize a closet, change the arrangement of vases and sculptures on her buffet, and sometimes even move furniture!

Now she knows the wisdom of separating these dissimilar events that require a different momentum from opposite sides of the brain. Cleaning follows rules in the left brain, and decorating is a creative procedure that activates the right side of the brain. So, when it's time to clean, simply clean!

I absolutely feel a sense of accomplishment when I have finished cleaning a room well. I always work from top to bottom, cleaning from the highest level of the room and working my way down to the floor. For example, I would dust a chandelier *before* dusting a tabletop; otherwise I would simply move the dust from the chandelier to the previously clean table.

While I clean, I play music that defines for me the perfect rhythm for cleaning—fast and furious—because it keeps me moving. It feels great to finally finish cleaning by dusting the accessories and replacing them in their perfectly beautiful, clean positions. The process of cleaning to the sound of music feels more complete and natural because it is rhythmic, engaging consistent areas of my brain. The process feels good to me because I have efficiently accomplished a task that also brings with it the emotional reward of a clean and pretty space.

Rhythm aids in the mastery or learning of a new task when both sides of the brain are needed to accomplish a task. Learning a new skill requires the ability to *monitor our progress* (using the creative side of the brain) as we are doing the task (using the left side of the brain). An example of this for me might be trying out a new creative painting technique while painting a room.

Most artistic painting techniques require mixing the proper ratio of paint versus glaze. This engages the scientific part of my brain versus the freely creative side. The creative side is involved in guiding the application of the mix artistically to accomplish the right finish. Combining two processes of science and artistic expressions creates a rhythm. If you add a little music to the equation, you enhance the experience and help your brain to learn the new technique at the same time.

By using both the scientific knowledge and the artistic gift of creativity, I experience a deeper satisfaction through the process than if I were simply changing paint colors in the room. As I move forward from wall to wall, I am forced to logically assess my skill of the new creative technique. Again, what makes this process most rewarding is the engagement of both sides of my brain.

The idea here is that we should be fully engaged in what we are doing at the moment rather than just acting like a robot as we work through a task. Listening to music involves a creative process of the brain that is not required for the repetitive motions of cleaning or painting. Adding two compatible processes that activate both sides of the brain increases the momentum of our productivity and pleasure.

Finally, the art of delegation is something that many people find difficult. But it too can help to streamline your activities and help you to accomplish more in a shorter period of time. The simplest tasks to delegate are those that you do not like to do yourself or that you are not good at doing. In many cases, it is both of those characteristics that inspire you to delegate. Delegating effectively is not just about getting the job done—it's about getting the job done well. And that requires giving the person to whom you have delegated the job the *authority* to make decisions that allow the job to be done in the best way possible.

If you are a control freak, you will struggle with this time-saver because it requires letting go of some of your own control and authority and giving it to someone else. For example, if you ask someone to clean your front walkway *once a week*—he will clean it once a week. However, if there is a huge storm and lots of leaves and other debris tumble down on your walkway—it may be nearly a week before it gets cleaned. If instead, you delegated the task of *keeping your front walk clean*, the worker would be more apt to clean it again after the storm even though he had already swept it earlier that week. So simply make clear what you want the end result to be, and then let the one to whom you have delegated the work decide how to accomplish it.

The best part of delegating is that everyone benefits from it. It helps us with our workloads, and it also helps others develop new skills and self-confidence. It creates an atmosphere of teamwork. As the team's self-confidence is built, we can delegate even more. In the end, sharing the workload causes everyone to win the prize of having more time for what we really want to do.

SIMPLICITY MADE SIMPLE

Here are some more tips for streamlining your workload:

Use the rule of **TALENT-BASED ORGANIZATION**. The most effective use of time requires wisely using individual talents to accomplish the given tasks. If someone has a perfectionist personality, then give her or him the assignment that requires just that kind of skill to achieve—like organizing your file system. She or he will enjoy the process and the project because it is something that will come easily and give great satisfaction in doing it.

IDENTIFY YOUR OWN STRENGTHS AND WEAKNESSES. Be as objective as you can. Then decide whether you want to spend more time learning a new skill in order to accomplish a task or whether it simply makes more sense to delegate it to someone who already has that skill. Remember, sometimes our greatest reward is in the process of learning. The ultimate decision should be based on the amount of time available to complete the task.

One key to **SUCCESSFUL DELEGATING** is to do it gradually. If you expect too much from someone all at once, you will only overwhelm him and discourage him from ever trying again. And that will not help you with your time schedule. Although you do want your team to be stretched a little beyond current abilities, you do not want to set them up to fail. Each new task should be built on the previous learned experience.

Avoid negating your own delegation by making decisions that the person now doing the job is capable of making. If you want to gain time by delegating, then you must **LET TEAM MEMBERS LEARN AND BE ENCOURAGED** by their own success. Sometimes, believe it or not, they may actually come up with a better way of doing things than we would have done ourselves. Give them that chance.

LEAVE ROOM FOR UNEXPECTED LESSONS. Sometimes our biggest lessons are the ones we learn through failure. Unless it is a matter of life and death, letting someone fail can often be the best teacher. Be sure that you are approachable, so that the person who has made a mistake feels comfortable and safe enough to actually come to you with the situation. We all make mistakes. When an error has been made, discuss how it could have been avoided and help him or her find a solution that will resolve the problem. This will help prevent a repeat incident and save time in the future.

SCHEDULE THINGS IN BLOCKS. When scheduling meetings or chores or errands, lump them all together rather than staggering them throughout the week. For example, in the spring I try to schedule all my annual checkups in close blocks of time. I may, for example, see my gynecologist and my eye doctor on the same day.

FOCUS ON THE PRESENT. Life can seem fleeting. Before we know it, we are older and wondering what happened to our lives. If we choose instead to be aware of the present, which is our lives, we will not need to wonder what happened to the time because we will still be happily experiencing it. Awareness is what makes life fulfilling. Awareness is what makes each moment an opportunity for creating importance and meaning. Rather than staying engaged in a conversation that is going nowhere, we can learn to be aware and make a choice to end the needless conversation that is interrupting our work, thereby creating our own rhythm. By *thinking*, we will become aware of what we are feeling and that will lead us to make better choices.

Lord, I will wisely reflect on the work I do, and I will listen for Your voice to lead me in ways to do it better. Thank You for keeping me from harm as I obey You.

The Madness of Multitasking

But I am afraid that just as Eve was deceived by the
serpent's cunning, your minds may somehow be led astray
from your sincere and pure devotion to Christ.

—2 CORINTHIANS 11:3 (NIV)

The Corinthians fell for smooth talkers delivering messages that sounded good and seemed to make sense. Today, we too could easily fall prey to the many false teachers and messages that appear on the surface to make sense. Just as we need to be cautious and search the Bible to check the teaching of someone who implies authority but tells us untruths, we need to apply these same checks-and-balances approaches to our daily living tasks. The Bible should be the final authority that we trust to guide and teach us.

When I started to research the topic of multitasking, I searched first in the Bible. This verse warned me to not be led astray. And it didn't take long to discover that the promise of a multitasking panacea is not the solution. Like so many things, it sounded too good to be true and it was. In the research for a study titled "Executive Control of Cognitive Processes in Task Switching"[19] (*whew*, that's quite a title!), it was determined that the subjects lost time when they had to switch from one task to another. In other words, people who are working on their computers while answering phones and talking to the person sitting next to them are being forced to switch gears constantly, instead of being able to take ten minutes and concentrate on one task at a time. The result is that, according to the technical reports, workers are losing twenty to forty percent of efficiency. In layman's terms—they can't concentrate and are not able to do any of the tasks to their best ability. As soon as they start working on something, they are forced to break their concentration and turn their attention elsewhere.

These days we are always looking for ways to accomplish more than one thing at a time. And one of the ways, driving while talking on the phone, is not only popular but controversial as well. Even a simple conversation can create the potential for an accident.

For example, if you talk to your husband on a cell phone while driving the car, you may be telling him to stop and get milk on his way home (which may seem like another time-saver, right?) but at the same time, you may also be trying to pay attention to traffic signals and read street signs while searching for an address that is unfamiliar. If you simply ignored your cell phone and turned off that distracting talk radio program, you could concentrate better and make sure you were paying attention to what you were doing.

Now, what would happen if during this simple conversation your husband informed you that he just found out he has to take a pay cut? Obviously, your brain would take a hard turn right toward that phone conversation using virtually all of your mental resources—now who's focusing on the driving? Not you, and that would not be good! Even if through this entire incident you were using a "no-hands" phone, you would still be asking your brain to manage a variety of activities. And you set yourself at great risk for an accident. It simply is not wise to engage in distracting conversations while driving, not even conversations with other passengers in the car.

TAKE TIME, SAVOR LIFE

Not all multitasking is bad. Some things are easier to combine into a multitasking situation. For me, I cannot write and listen to music at the same time. The music is simply too distracting for me. For someone else, it may be soothing and provide just the inspiration they need. I can, however, listen to music while I pay bills. What's the difference? I don't know, I just know it is the way it works for me. Some kids say they can actually do homework while listening to or watching television. I could never do that either. And it makes me wonder if they are really telling the truth.

The bottom line is that multitasking forces us to focus our conscious awareness in more than one place at a time. And although it may seem like a way to save time, it really depends what the task is. Jobs that we can almost do in our sleep probably allow us to multitask—unlike those that require more concentration. In our attempt to accomplish more in less time, we simply have to be careful about what activities we combine.

Guideposts writer Lee Webber wrote about an experience she had regarding the hustle and bustle of the life we live:

> As I was walking through our public library, my eyes fell on the "How-To" section of records and tapes. The one that caught my attention was entitled "How to Hustle."

Oh no! I thought. That's exactly what I do not need. I have hustled all my life! I wonder how much I have missed because I was always in a hurry!

Just that morning a young man had impatiently sped by me on the road in a mad rush to get to wherever he was going, but when I got to the next traffic light, here he was! He hadn't gained a thing.

I saw myself in that fellow. I've always lived a "shoe-horn" life—trying to squeeze in one more thing. "Need another board member? I'll do it!" "A little league manager? I can handle that." "Someone to sing in the quartet? You can count on me." I zoomed from meeting to practice to rehearsal week after week. Needless to say, I was exhausted.

So I prayed, "Lord, slow me down." And He did. He's taught me about time through my clock-making hobby. As I design a clock casing, as I cut the wood, as I position the clock mechanism, I'm reminded that humans, not God, invented these devices for measuring time.

With that in mind, I no longer allow myself to be run by the clock. I take time to play with my granddaughter Trace and learn new things about the world through her inquisitive mind. Morning walks with my wife Peg now give us reflection time together, instead of being preoccupied with organizing my day. I even chew my food more slowly, savoring the delicate tastes hidden in a casserole or stew. And sometimes I'll pray by saying nothing—just sitting with God in peace and quiet. I'd say I've stopped hustling all right.[20]

What Lee learned is that unless we give the individual tasks in our lives more attention rather than less, we will miss the best part, like the rich flavor of home-baked apple pie. You can eat it standing up while talking on the phone in the midst of packing lunches—or you can take ten minutes to sit down and savor the flavor of life. The choice is yours.

No matter the research or the scientific evidence, we are all still unique individuals with different talents and abilities. The key is in knowing our limitations and, of course, consulting with our personal time-management consultant—God!

SIMPLICITY MADE SIMPLE

Here are some tips to help you decide when multitasking makes sense for you:

Be aware of how our brains have learned when to tune out and what to tune in as part of the process of multitasking. **SPEND SOME TIME PRACTICING AWARENESS.** Try experimenting with a voluntary selective process. Place a rubber band on your wrist and when you notice it is there throughout your day, tune in to what you are doing at that moment. Pay attention also to what is going on around you. Did you notice anything you might have missed had you not decided to be aware?

RECOGNIZE THAT MEN AND WOMEN DIFFER IN THEIR ABILITY TO MULTITASK. An article in *Research* says men's brains are programmed differently than women's and, as a result, women multitask better. Redefine your expectations regarding your husband's ability to multitask. In other words, expect less.

MULTITASKING WHILE ON THE PHONE is probably something we all do. The key to being successful is to be mindful of who you are talking to. Some people, or conversation topics, simply require more concentration than others. Also, don't try to do something "new" while talking on the phone. It's okay to prepare your infamous meatloaf while carrying on a phone conversation, but this is not the time to try out the new grill.

BE FORGIVING OF YOURSELF AND YOUR LIMITATIONS. Our brains can multitask in ways that are extremely beneficial. For example, if you live in a noisy area, perhaps near an airport or highway, your brain learns to filter out that noise. The brain becomes selective in what it hears. This frees up your brain, so you can concentrate and save time by being able to focus on your work despite the noise. But sometimes the world simply gets too noisy and too crowded, and we hit overload. Learn to recognize when you hit the overload stage and begin to simplify your expectations.

UNDERSTAND YOUR BRAIN and use it well. Studies suggest that humans may be the only species that can perform a type of multitasking called *branching*. Branching allows us to keep a specific goal in mind over time (working memory), while at the same time being able to change focus among tasks (attentional resource allocation). This can be helpful for planning your special grouping of tasks. Preparing Thanksgiving dinner is a good example of branching. While you keep the overall goal of getting the turkey cooked and on the table, you prepare all the side dishes in the meantime.

USE AN ACTIVITY JOURNAL to help evaluate your ability to multitask. Consider your use of time and your energy level at different times of the day. I know that my most productive time of day is morning. Don't ask me to perform anything brainy after 4:00 P.M. The journal will help give you some insight as to how much you can handle. Then you decide which tasks should be combined, dropped, delayed or delegated.

USE YOUR WAIT TIME. While waiting in lines you can reconfirm appointments (a good time to use your cell phone), catch up on reading, or make a list of important upcoming events for which you want to prepare.

> Lord, I will be more sensitive to the single task that
> You set before me. I will savor each moment and work
> when it is time to work, rest when it is time to rest,
> and play when it is time to laugh.

Sleep like a Baby

To every thing there is a season,

and a time to every purpose under the heaven.

—ECCLESIASTES 3:1 (KJV)

Solomon's point in this verse is that God has a plan for all of us. He provides specific cycles of life, each with its own purpose. Timing is important. The secret to living a happy, peaceful life is to discover God's plan and do it in God's timing. God wants us to enjoy life and without proper rest, we simply will not.

Our natural internal body clock is called our circadian rhythm. It regulates when our bodies get sleepy and when it's time to wake up. Our circadian clock operates on a twenty-four- to twenty-five-hour schedule that is directly affected by light. The German word for light is *zeitgeber*, which means time-giver. This is the perfect description because light is what sets our biological circadian clock. In a perfect world, we would all go to bed when it got dark and rise when it got light. But no, we modern and sophisticated people have learned how to beat the clock by using electric light to extend the daylight and thus we have simultaneously managed to deprive ourselves of sleep. We are brilliant!

We were designed to operate somewhat like a battery that needs to be recharged on a regular basis. Although no one seems to be sure why we sleep, there is certainly a lot of information about sleep, or our lack of it. What we know for sure is that we need sleep. Most of us need seven to eight-and-a-half hours a night. It is the timing of our sleep that is critical. When our schedules are erratic or we attempt to alter our routine is when we will most likely find ourselves unable to sleep well. We may, for example, have trouble falling asleep or staying asleep or simply not sleeping well.

Most of us experience a sleep disorder of this nature at one time or another. Our circadian rhythms can be affected by almost any kind of outside stimulus. Sometimes someone simply turning on the light after you have fallen asleep will be enough to disrupt the rest of the night. Working shift work, or split shifts, or jet lag can all create a long-term disruption in your normal sleep pattern.

I work split shifts at QVC (the television shopping channel). This weekend I have a midnight show, a 4:00 A.M. show, and a 3:00 P.M. show. My poor body will not be happy. So what can I do to help it keep up? Experts recommend that I try to take a four-hour nap sometime in the middle of the night (or during what would be my normal sleep time). By sleeping through at least half of the time usually reserved for sleep, the circadian rhythm remains anchored or stable. My only chance for this nap will be after my 4:00 A.M. show. If I were getting off work at 8:00 A.M., then experts say to take a four-hour nap at that point and wake up at noon. The goal is to give your body enough sleep to keep going but not so much that you are not able to go to sleep at your regular time that evening.

Some people consider themselves to be morning people, while others think of themselves as night owls. What makes the difference is the time our body temperature peaks. For those who go to bed early and get up early, our temperature usually peaks before noon. Evening people have their temperature peak later in the second half of the day. Our body temperature drops during sleep. If we get our circadian cycle out of whack, it can take as long as a week to get back to normal.

TAKE TIME TO RECHARGE YOURSELF

Our memory is sharpest after restorative sleep. There are two stages to sleep: REM (Rapid Eye Movement) and non-REM, or deep sleep.[21] Contrary to popular belief, REM is not when we get the most restorative sleep. REM is often filled with dreams that keep us moving. Non-REM is when the restoration happens. Non-REM actually has four phases. Delta wave is the fourth stage and that is when we are in the deepest sleep. Delta wave is when our bodies have the lowest metabolic activity and our muscles are relaxed, our blood pressure lowers, and our pulse rates slow. This critical stage of sleep is also when growth hormones reach their peak. In addition, it's when the blood supply to the muscles is increased and tissue grows and repair occurs. Our immune system also rejuvenates during this cycle. When you think about all that occurs during just this sleep cycle, it's no wonder we feel like garbage when we don't get a good night's sleep!

I found a fine poem by Guideposts author Fred Bauer that describes how we all have felt at one time and how we all can have hope for peaceful rest.

"For Restless Sleeper"
Trouble-filled, I toss and turn,
Like curdled milk in butter churn,
My rest is clouded by worries vague,

Faceless demons a night-long plague,
Sleep that's robbed by fears unfounded,
Cries for faith that's in God grounded,
Alas I beg His intervention,
"Release me from this unnamed tension,"
And in the grip of darkest hour,
He reassures with sovereign power . . .
Be not anxious in any way,
Place tomorrow with yesterday,
They're both the same, don't you see,
Equal in reality,
Only this moment really counts
And only lasting faith surmounts,
Trust is all I need to carry
You through trials of which you're wary,
Now close your eyes and go to sleep,
Your soul's securely in My keep.[22]

When we finally learn to budget our time, plan our schedules well, stay enthusiastic, and rest when we are tired, time will seem more abundant and our outlook on life is certain to improve.

S I M P L I C I T Y   M A D E   S I M P L E

Here are some ideas that can help you get your sleep schedule back on track:

LEARN TO MAKE UP FOR LOST SLEEP when your schedule robs you of a full night of rest. Adults operate best on eight to eight-and-a-half hours of sleep each night, although some people seem able to exist on as little as five hours and others need ten hours. Sleeping too little causes "sleep debt" and, contrary to popular belief, you can make up sleep—but only to a degree. The best way to repay this debt is to readjust by sleeping long periods over the next few days.

RULE OUT PHYSICAL CAUSES FOR SLEEP INTERRUPTION AND ADJUST FOR YOUR AGE. Old age does affect sleep, but not the way we most often think. Older people tend to sleep more lightly and for shorter periods of time. However, the time spent in delta wave reduces. Making up the difference and getting the restorative sleep that is needed requires an increase in the total duration of sleep time. Unfortunately, it takes older folks longer to fall asleep, and they often wake up during the night. Sleep fragmentation can also be aggravated by other medical conditions such as sleep apnea, muscle pain and cardiopulmonary problems that make sleeping a sometimes frustrating activity. By addressing these physical ailments, we can finally get a good night's sleep.

PAY ATTENTION TO TELLTALE SIGNS that you are not getting the rest you need. Evaluate your alertness and reaction time. Lack of sleep affects both. Delayed sleep (or sleep latency) is the measure of how quickly you get to sleep. If you are falling asleep as soon as you lay down, it could be an indicator of extreme fatigue and sleep deprivation. How's your mood? It's not a good sign if you find yourself waking up cranky. A good night's sleep should leave you refreshed. And a very, very bad sign is if you have one of those "how did I get here?" moments. That is called a microsleep, which is a period of up to thirty seconds of sleep that you did not even know you took!

STOP YOUR MIND FROM RACING. If you are like me, the minute you go to bed, your mind starts to race. The simplest way to solve this sleep dilemma is to get up and write down what you are thinking or worrying about. But do this with a minimum of light. Bright light will stimulate you and make you more awake.

DON'T COUNT SHEEP. The fact is that those who count sheep take longer to fall asleep. Experts recommend that you visualize a waterfall, a quiet beach or some other relaxing place.

Accept the fact that there simply will be some days when your energy level is off. Rather than trying to stick to your normal routine, give yourself a break and take some time for a **PERSONAL RECUPERATION DAY**. Your old self will be glad and ready to return to normal soon.

> Lord, when I lie down, I will not be afraid;
> my sleep will be sweet because I have no fear
> of sudden disaster or of ruin, for You are
> my confidence and I know You will keep me safe.

PART THREE

The Gracefulness of Time

THERE IS A GRACEFULNESS to time that can be enjoyed; it is found in activities that are worth repeating, activities that become traditions or rituals. Planning for family celebrations is worth the investment that must be made, but giving a portion of our time to benefit the lives of others reaps a reward too. Wisdom makes time more graceful, and it can be both learned and shared through time spent with other people. If we learn to focus our time on what is good and pure and lovely, a satisfied life awaits us.

The Balance of Rituals

And the Lord called unto Moses, and spake unto him out

of the tabernacle of the congregation, saying, Speak unto

the children of Israel, and say unto them, If any man of

you bring an offering unto the Lord, ye shall bring your

offering of the cattle, even of the herd, and of the flock.

—LEVITICUS 1:1 (KJV)

When reading the book of Leviticus it is easy to simply dismiss it as a long record of "weird" rituals. Although the rituals may seem peculiar and out of place today, the practices made sense to the people of that time, and they offer great insight for us into God's nature and character. When the Israelites saw the sacrificial animals, they became more aware of and sensitive to the destructiveness of their own sins represented in the shed blood of the animals. The ritual reminded them that the wage of their sins is death.

But the purpose of the ritual was also to reveal to us a forgiving and holy God Who should be loved and worshipped. The laws were to help keep us from sinning, and sacrifices were meant to bring out a heartfelt devotion to God when we saw that He accepted a substitute for our transgressions. Consequently, the ceremonies and rituals were the best way to bring the Israelites to focusing their hearts on Him.

A few years ago, when my nephew returned from four years away in the Navy, we were all excited to hear about the new and wonderful places he had seen. We expected him, like our uncle before him, to be so enchanted with a faraway place that he would soon want to travel again. But my nephew's response was very different; all his journeys made him realize how much home really meant to him. He said, "All I want is to be able to spend every Christmas at Grandma's." Of course, we were puzzled and thought it was a strange remark. But he went on to explain that Christmas at Grandma's was special. No matter what, my nephew knew he could count on the consistency and the familiarity of the pattern (ritual) that was set for the celebration.

He knew, for example, that all the young children would be allowed to open just one gift—the one from their godparent—on Christmas Eve. This was special. He knew that Grandma's infamous cookies, nut roll and poppy seed roll would be part of the celebration. He knew that we would sing, laugh and even cry as we looked back over the year. He knew we would rejoice together over the good things and encourage each other to let go of the bad. For my nephew, this holiday ceremony was a major brick in the foundation of his life. He simply could not imagine moving far away and missing this family ritual.

I don't think any of us ever thought about our Christmas celebration as being a ritual, yet it perfectly fits a definition from wordIQ.com (online): "The general purpose of rituals is to express some fundamental truth or meaning, evoke spiritual, numinous emotional responses from participants, and/or engage a group of people in unified action to strengthen their communal bonds." We often think of ritual as being associated only with a worship service and with a close connection to reverence. But outside of worship, rituals can have a much more basic social function by reinforcing shared values and beliefs. Rituals can range from grand ceremonies to simple everyday events—like lighting a candle at dinner. That small gesture can turn an ordinary dinner into something special.

Creating rituals is a relatively simple way to organize our time and bring significance and remembrance to our lives. You can, for example, develop a ritual for graduation. That way, whenever someone graduates, he or she receives the gift of the tradition. Our family always celebrates birthdays at Grandma's (my mom's) and we always have date-nut cake—whether you like it or not. (Most of us do.)

Daily rituals can benefit those of us who are getting older. For example, as our nests empty, we lose the anchor that our children brought to our daily lives. We can feel a bit lost for lack of structure without the demands, or ritual, that caring for young children require, or the routine of a full-time work schedule. Creating our own chosen form of discipline becomes more important, and rituals can help us manage our time well.

As a child I remember seeing three older women in church during the middle of the day—each quietly praying. Every week, three times a week, they would come. I was so awed by their devotion. For them, this ritual kept them connected to God. It was a discipline of their time that came from the repetition of it.

The benefit of aging is having more time to spend on our spiritual life. A ritual that is associated with our faith can make it stronger and be our new daily anchor. By setting a specific time and day—for prayer, fasting or journaling—we create a ritual that brings new meaning to our lives.

Some rituals simply keep our schedules on track. My friend Jan always does her laundry on Mondays. She works the rest of her schedule around that particular task. It is a simple way of making sure that she has clean clothes when she needs them. Near the end of the week, she knows exactly what is still clean and what her options are. It makes deciding what to wear easier. Other rituals, like being sure our checks get deposited into our checking account on time, simply make financial planning easier. Still others, like walking several times a week with a friend, can improve our physical and emotional well-being.

SIMPLICITY MADE SIMPLE

As you think about ways that rituals can make a difference in your life, here are some ideas to consider:

PLAN AN "ALL-IN-ONE" BIRTHDAY CELEBRATION. If your family is scattered throughout the country, why not celebrate everyone's birthday once or twice a year? Everyone whose birthday is in the first half of the year celebrates together and then the second half celebrates together. It's a wonderful way to make it easy for the family to get together for a reunion and still make birthdays special.

TAME YOUR SCHEDULE WITH A MONTHLY VIEW. How often have you said, "Where did the month go?" Our schedules can either look the same month to month or simply be so full that we miss opportunities to spend time doing things we really want to do. Consider the month of December, for example. You certainly want to set aside time to celebrate with your family. But you may also want to take a field trip with your grandkids during their Christmas vacation. Or perhaps you'd like to plan a day of ice skating or take your grandson to a professional hockey game. These are all things that don't automatically fall into your normal routine. They require planning. Now is the time (while you are thinking about it) to pull out your December calendar and add these wish-list items to it.

MAKE TRAVEL PLANS. Perhaps you enjoy winter vacations. I only like winter vacations if they involve someplace warm! However, unless I take the time to plan a vacation early, I will never get away. My husband and I like to sail with friends. It takes a lot of planning for four of us to clear our schedules for two weeks, plan our meals, make travel arrangements and "get our acts together." So we only plan this major trip once every two years. That is our ritual. Whatever your family's interests or hobbies are, you will reduce the stress by planning for them far in advance and thereby ensure that everyone has a good time.

TAKE INTO ACCOUNT YOUR FAMILY'S INTERESTS. If there are particular hobbies, contests, classes or even conventions that you enjoy, add them into your schedule. Whether it means becoming a regular ticket holder for the local symphony or checking the schedule of your favorite tour group, the only way to enjoy the rewards of the occasion is to actually attend—and that means blocking off time in your schedule. My mom always gets tickets to the theatre and then invites one of her grandchildren to each of the several shows based on each child's special interests. By doing this early, ahead of the season, everyone is able to keep this date.

PLAN SOME TIME FOR A LITTLE LIFE IN THE SLOW LANE. As we all live on the verge of exhaustion, our bodies are struggling to keep up. Our minds . . . well, let's just say I think I lose mine several times a day when I'm in the midst of a rush. Unless we plan for some "downtime," we will never catch up. My friend Jan makes sure her schedule is free to watch Oprah everyday. This is her downtime for rest and relaxation. A little "R & R" will make you happier, healthier and more productive. Choose a time each day in your schedule to simply slow down—and make it your ritual date with yourself.

REDUCE MENTAL CLUTTER. Learn to focus on the present by scheduling your tasks. Then, rather than wondering or worrying about when you will find the time to accomplish the things that need doing, you will be able to relax knowing that you have planned and set aside the time you need. The added bonus is that by writing down in your calendar a committed amount of time for the task, you gain the motivation needed to actually do it.

> Lord, each day as I enjoy the ritual of eating bread and
> drinking from Your rich provision, I will remember that
> Christ, the perfect Lamb of God, was sacrificed
> as a substitute for my sins, and I will take time
> to give thanks for all You have done for me.

Tithing Your Time

And above all things have fervent charity among
yourselves: for charity shall cover the multitude of sins.

—1 PETER 4:8 (KJV)

Ultimately, how we live our lives matters in God's kingdom. Our lives should be a perpetual preparation for meeting our King. Those preparations include continually growing in our love for Him and for others. Not only is it important that we regularly pray, but also that we reach out to those less fortunate than ourselves. Our possessions, status and power will mean nothing in God's kingdom. So we should invest them here on earth where they will make a difference.

Regardless of your personal financial situation you can make a difference by tithing your time and talents to serve the Lord. We should give lovingly because God loved us first, and He created us to love Him back. If we believe that all we have belongs to Him, then we understand that giving our time to others is simply a way to give back to God what rightfully belongs to Him in the first place. And just think of the exciting opportunities you will experience by making this simple investment of your time! Second Corinthians 8:7 (NIV) tells us to "excel in this grace of giving." This should encourage us to give more joyfully of our time.

EXCEL IN THE GRACE OF GIVING TIME

The idea of tithing applies perfectly to time. Of course, we all know that there is always more than one way to calculate our tithes—right? Let's start with the ten percent tithing rule. Using the forty-hour work week, ten percent would equal four hours a week—a manageable amount of time. Okay, now how many hours are you awake each day—don't cheat. I'm usually awake sixteen hours. If I used that number as my base calculation, then I would need to tithe 11.2 hours a week. Now that's a lot of time. But just imagine the possibilities of what could be accomplished in your church, your community or for your family if you actually took that much time from your schedule and gave it as a tithe.

Fred Bauer wrote about an amazing woman and her gift of time tithing:

> When I was a young man on my first job as a newspaper reporter, I was required to write obituaries, one of the lowliest assignments a writer can get. But I found people's life stories fascinating, because they were full of art-of-living lessons. To this day I read obituaries with appreciation.
>
> One of my recent favorites was the obituary of Gladys Holm of Evanston, Illinois. On the surface she seemed a rather ordinary woman. Oh, she liked bright-red suits, drove a red Cadillac, and was generous to friends and relatives, but she

lived in a tiny apartment and remained single all her life. Born on a farm in Wisconsin to immigrant parents, she moved to Chicago at age eighteen and went to work for a small hospital supply company, serving the firm's founder as a secretary.

When the business went public, Gladys was given stock options and was named to the executive committee. The company grew and eventually was absorbed by a larger one, and Gladys retired. But she didn't sit down; she continued doing volunteer work at Children's Memorial Hospital where she had, over the years, become a fixture.

Known as the "Teddy Bear Lady," she brought smiles to hundreds of sick children by giving them stuffed animals. If hospital bills were a problem for a family, she quietly contributed from what was thought to be her meager pension and savings. Her job never paid more than fifteen thousand dollars a year. That's why friends were amazed when she died at age eighty-six and left fifteen million dollars to the hospital for medical research. Her stock had grown manifold, and there was only one place she wanted it to go: to children.

As a tribute to Gladys, the hospital held a memorial service a few weeks after her death. When the guests arrived, they found at each chair something that made them smile: one of her trademark teddy bears.

And that's why I read obituaries.[23]

That is an amazing story. But even if Gladys had never left a dime to the hospital—the gift of her time would have been equally memorable. Tithing is a matter of the heart. If we have no income, we can still give from our other abundances. We can give of our time, our resources and our talents. God blesses us and provides for us. We have an obligation to bless others as God has blessed us.

I read with interest a story in our local newspaper about the volunteer organization Experience Corps, based in Washington, D.C.[24] The article, originally published by the *Wall Street Journal*, explained that this nonprofit group specialized in tutoring young students using volunteers that are fifty years or older. The point of the story is that this is an extremely successful program.

Unlike so many other volunteer programs, in this one these older volunteers always show up on time and never get bored with the work. Their organization has sidestepped these two pitfalls of volunteer programs by expecting more of its volunteers—more time and work, and more commitment. The organization knows they need the help of their volunteers, but they still place high expectations on the quality of the work. Consequently, the people who volunteer for this organization consider their positions to be a job—a big job. As a result, people feel more respected and love the challenge. The fact that the volunteers *know* they are making a difference makes this program unique. This is excelling in the grace of giving (2 Corinthians 8:7).

SIMPLICITY MADE SIMPLE

Here are some other ideas to help you get started with tithing your time:

Simply **GIVE WITH A PURE AND OPEN HEART**, and you will share a part of yourself. This makes your gift available as an instrument of Christ. It is true charity. When you give of your heart you inspire others, and anything is possible.

Take the time to **FIGURE OUT HOW YOUR GOD-GIVEN TALENTS CAN HELP** your church, community or other nonprofit organizations. Then determine to tithe with all your heart and with as much time as you can give.

TO GET, YOU HAVE TO GIVE. Malachi 3:10 (NIV) says, "Bring the whole tithe into the storehouse, that there may be food in my house. Test me in this," says the Lord Almighty, "and see if I will not throw open the floodgates of heaven and pour out so much blessing that you will not have room enough for it."

KEEP TRACK OF HOW YOU SPEND YOUR DAY. This is a great way to evaluate the stewardship of your time. Record, for example, the number of hours you slept, worked, or spent time on devotional/study and Christian service. Be sure to include commuting time, recreational time, social time, laundry, exercise, hobbies and miscellaneous time spent. Then add up the hours to evaluate your stewardship.

THINK OF GOOD DEEDS AS AN OBLIGATION. When King Solomon began building the great Temple in Jerusalem, he led a campaign not for material or financial contributions—but for workers. This is a good example of the traditionally Jewish attitude toward giving of both money and time. The Jewish word *mitzvah* is a commandment that can only be fulfilled with a good deed performed out of religious duty. Unlike the word *charity*, which we perceive as optional rather than required, the performance of a mitzvah is an obligation of an entirely different character. We can never falter in our contribution of time and money if we view these gifts as our obligation (mitzvah) to our Lord. This is one Jewish law that we all should follow.

GIVE TIME TO SHARE YOUR FAITH WITH OTHERS—even when it's not convenient or you don't think you have the time. Second Timothy 4:2 (NLT) says "Be persistent, whether the time is favorable or not." We are to be good stewards of our time and money even when it is not convenient and especially when all the temptations of our busy lives get in the way—we are to persist. Our persistence is a mark of a true follower of Christ.

BE STRONG AND HAVE SELF-CONTROL. Self-control takes strength and courage. The apostle Paul assures us that we have been given all the courage we need to do God's work. He wrote: "For God did not give us a spirit of timidity—of cowardice, of craven and cringing and fawning fear—but [He has given us a spirit] of power and of love and of calm and well-balanced mind and discipline and self-control" (2 Timothy 1:7, AMP).

BE FAITHFUL. Paul wrote, "It is required that those who have been given a trust must prove faithful" (1 Corinthians 4:2, NIV). Faithfulness is being dependable. A dependable person is someone we can count on to be steady every day. A trustworthy steward will evaluate his opportunities every day and invest what God has given him in a way that will produce the best possible results.

> Lord, I want to excel in the grace of giving. Show me ways to offer my time so that You are glorified and others are served on Your behalf.

Bartering Your Time

Wisdom is the principal thing; therefore get wisdom:

and with all thy getting get understanding.

—PROVERBS 4:7 (KJV)

David taught Solomon as a young boy that seeking God's wisdom was the most important thing he could do. Solomon learned his lesson well. When God appeared to the new king and offered to fulfill any request, Solomon chose wisdom and knowledge above all else (2 Chronicles 1:7–12). We shouldn't sit waiting for God to appear to us before we ask Him for wisdom. Instead, it is something we should boldly pray about every day. And sometimes God's answer for wisdom comes to us through someone else's help.

One of my clients took on a home-remodeling project that was way over his head. (You know, the kind of project that you would expect to take two weeks and then before you know it, three months have gone by. And to make matters worse, not only did you lose a colossal amount of time, but the outcome was not exactly as you pictured it.) He was determined to take on the process of refinishing the wood floors in his living and dining rooms. I admired his courage and thought, *Wow, he must be talented.*

Several months went by before I heard from him again. (He was waiting for all the new furniture to arrive so I could see the finished room.) Finally, he invited me out to see the refinished floors. They were gorgeous. They shined, they were smooth, and the finish was even throughout—quite a feat for a beginner. As I complimented him on his amazing work, he got a twinkle in his eye and then said, "Thanks for the compliment—the floors do look great—but I didn't do them alone."

This man is not only honest, but he is also wise. He hired his experienced neighbor as his boss/assistant for the floor-refinishing project. The results were spectacular—the floor project was finished in less than two weeks, the job was as good as it could be, and my client learned a new craft—all in the same time.

LEARNING FROM OTHERS SAVES TIME

Working alongside an experienced teacher saves us countless hours that would be wasted in wrong turns, as well as time spent repairing botched projects. The idea of swapping expertise to gain skill and save time (as well as money) is a wonderful approach that simply makes sense. Think of it as bartering, an idea as old as mankind. When you barter, you trade for services or goods—you simply pay for them with something other than money. It's a win-win situation.

Just think of all the skills, knowledge, faith and philosophies that get passed on from one generation to the next. Cultures, too, pass from one generation to another. Here in Lancaster, Pennsylvania, the Amish teach their children their cultural skills by letting them work alongside someone who is experienced. They even passed a law that gives exception to the child labor laws—so that the Amish boys could go into the sawmills to learn their trade. (The law previously said that no one under the age of eighteen was allowed.)

Sometimes to be a good steward of the time and talent God has given us, we have to take a risk. Guideposts writer Terry Helwig wrote the following story about such a time:

> I stood knee-deep in the ocean, my thoughts swirling like the foaming water around me. For some time I had been incubating the idea of going back to school, maybe to become a counselor or therapist. But at forty-one, becoming a student again would mean many changes: new schedules, new demands, new courage. Was I capable of such a demanding challenge?
>
> I squinted my eyes, looking at the sandy bottom below the surface. Something tumbled against my right foot. Was it a murex shell? I bent down and grabbed a fistful of sand. Aha! I felt the rough grooves of the murex in my fingertips.
>
> As I studied it in the morning sunlight, I saw two round eyes, peering out at me. The shell had become a home for a hermit crab. I opened my palm wide. Its two large claws cautiously emerged, then its dark eyes, and finally its whole upper body. I remembered reading that hermit crabs twist their bodies into the spiral of empty seashells. As they grow, they shed their shell for a larger one.
>
> I looked at it. How did it know when to find a bigger shell? Was it scary letting go of the old? As I lowered the crab into the water, I wished it well on its journey of living. And I

prayed that when the time came, I too would have the courage to leave my little space in search of a new one . . . roomy enough for growth and change.

P.S. That fall, I began to act on my dream. I sent for some college catalogs, attended interviews, and in the spring I began my first semester at Regis University in Denver, Colorado.[25]

Some schools will even let us barter our life experience for credit toward a degree. That's a sure way to save time!

SIMPLICITY MADE SIMPLE

Here are some thoughts to help you decide when and how it makes sense for you to swap expertise for time:

All young mothers need a day off. A simple solution is to **SWAP CHILD CARE ONE DAY** a week with another mom whose children are similar in age to yours. By doing this, both mothers gain a day of independence for running errands, cleaning house or simply taking a well-needed day off.

Use something you love to do as **YOUR BARGAINING CHIP**. My sister *loves* to clean and paint—bless her heart. Anyway, she often exchanges cleaning for other services such as home repairs or tax preparation.

If you want to improve in any area or skill, **SPEND TIME WITH OTHERS WHO KNOW MORE,** or are better at it than you are. It's a great way to learn and save time. We can draw from a wealth of possible teachers. Coaches, trainers, teachers, professors, support groups, discussion groups and many others can help us improve in many different ways.

You will save time and learn more quickly if you **KNOW HOW YOU LEARN**. Not everyone learns the same way. Each of us has a unique learning style—which means some of us are better suited to specific tasks than others. There are three basic styles of learning: visual, auditory and tactile/kinesthetic. I am visual. I see a picture in my mind. For example, I need to write down things so I can *see* what I'm to remember. When I was in college, if I took good notes, then I could literally call up the picture of my notes in my brain and see a visual of them. When I needed a particular answer, I simply scrolled down in my brain to the location where my notes gave the answer. If I simply sat in class and listened, I could not remember a thing.

LISTEN AND LEARN. Auditory learners are blessed with the ability to simply listen and learn. If you play music by ear, you are an auditory learner. I have never been able to put two notes together without sheet music in front of me. I simply am not able to learn this way.

FEEL YOUR WAY TO LEARNING. Tactile/kinesthetic learners literally feel their way. If, for example, you dial a phone without looking—this is probably your learning style. There is a subtle difference between tactile and kinesthetic. Tactile learners learn best through their sense of touch—using their hands and fingers. They learn best by writing, drawing, taking notes and using hands-on manipulatives while involving their emotions and feeling through the learning process. Kinesthetic learners learn best through the movement of larger motor muscles. For example, role-playing, real-life activities, or writing on a flip chart or chalkboard to learn.

MATCH YOUR LEARNING STYLE TO YOUR LESSON. When we understand our particular style of learning, it makes the process much simpler and less stressful. When someone tries to teach me something new, I absolutely must take the time at each step to write out the instructions. It can be frustrating because many people simply want to *show* me or *tell* me how to do it. I have tried the "watch me" approach and have never successfully been able to duplicate their action. If I am able to write out the instructions *and* watch—then I have a double advantage of two visual aids. The key to successful learning is finding strategies that work for *you* based on your own style of learning.

APPRECIATE DIFFERENCES. We add strength and depth to our lives when we bring together diverse skills, backgrounds and experiences; this is diversity at its best. Each person can contribute a positive influence, a different perspective and new ideas for solving problems. This is God's idea of community working together for the benefit of all. As we learn from each other, we expand our horizons physically, emotionally, timewise and spiritually.

> Lord, please give me the wisdom to know
> when it's time to ask for help and the humility
> needed to receive help when it is offered to me.

Life Satisfaction

All the days of the oppressed are wretched,

but the cheerful heart has a continual feast.

—PROVERBS 15:15 (NIV)

W hat is a cheerful heart? How can I get a cheerful heart if I don't have one? This verse tells us that our attitude can color our whole personality. Although we certainly cannot always choose what time serves to us, we can choose our attitude toward it. And those who adopt a more cheerful attitude toward life are the most satisfied people. The secret to adopting a cheerful attitude is to fill our minds with thoughts that are true, pure and lovely—thoughts that allow us to dwell on the good things in life.

Our personal sense of satisfaction in life is affected by many different factors. While the factors vary somewhat for each individual circumstance and personality, some factors are consistent in terms of rating life satisfaction. The factors that most highly correlate with life contentment as a whole are satisfaction in marriage, our work and our sense of purpose. In other words, the people who feel most content in these three areas are the ones that feel most satisfied with life in general.

Not surprisingly, those who take time to attend church on a regular basis are more satisfied in many areas of their lives than those people who do not attend church. In addition, those who attend church are more satisfied with their standard of living, regardless of whether they are satisfied with their income or overall financial situation. Church attendees are also more satisfied with their marriages and their sex lives. *Hmm . . .* I guess there must be something to this church thing! And the number one factor for satisfaction is one's sense of purpose in life. In other words, if we spend our time being in God's will, doing God's will, we will be delightfully satisfied with our lives.

Filling our minds with thoughts that are true, pure, and lovely and dwelling on the good things in life includes doing things that we find enjoyable and satisfying. As women, we spend most of our lives making sure that those around us are cared for, happy and doing the things they want to do; we naturally sacrifice for the good of the family. But at some point, we have to take the time to reclaim a little bit of life for ourselves. Unless we do, we will never find the time to dwell on those good things in our lives.

TAKE TIME TO CHEER UP

This task of dwelling on good things is compounded when we no longer even remember what things we enjoyed doing—let alone feel as though we can take the time to do them. Finding and committing time to doing something that seems so superfluous can feel a bit self-indulgent. But collecting our thoughts and taking the time to nurture ourselves can bring contentment and much-needed satisfaction to the rest of our lives. Remember, God rested on the Sabbath. He took time for Himself—and you should too. As we gain more satisfaction in our lives from the simple task of doing something that satisfies us, we learn to have a cheerful attitude that leads to a cheerful heart. When our hearts are cheerful, all of life seems better.

Sometimes the satisfaction comes from unexpected activities. Believe it or not, I get satisfaction out of ironing—especially my bed linens. A restful Sunday afternoon for me is having the time to iron my sheets! I love the smell, the touch and the way they look after being pressed. When I crawl into bed at night, it makes me feel wonderful. My friend Deb finds it therapeutic to bake. Her family and friends don't need all the pies she makes, but mixing and rolling dough relaxes her. A good weekend is one in which Deb has time to bake. By taking a little time to do these simple tasks we are celebrating life and enjoying it. Guideposts writer Carol Knapp wrote a story about how she improved her own life satisfaction:

> Last January I went through a terrible three-week depression. Alaska is cold and dark this time of year, which is enough to sabotage anybody's good mood. But there was more to it than that. With the children all out of the nest—and our oldest, Tamara, just married—I found myself wondering who I really was and where my life had gone. One afternoon I stood staring into the mirror, my face red and swollen from crying, calling out to the stranger in the glass, "Who are you? I don't know you."
>
> During those bleak days, I buried myself at home. I vowed to get out of Alaska the next January, if that would keep the depression from happening again. Finally, with the arrival of out-of-town guests, I began to pick up my life once more.

Several months later, I listened to a "Celebrate Life" tape by Luci Swindoll. She advised, "Be involved. While you can, say yes to more things than you say no to." I re-inventoried my January melancholy and realized I had said yes to very little. I didn't meet with friends, complete projects, work out at the gym, volunteer at church or reach out to anyone in any way. My life was one great big "no."

January is here again. This time around I'm going to try out a lot more yesses and see where that lands me. Maybe I won't need to leave the state. Maybe there is joy in my own backyard. Even in January.[26]

In Carol's case, not taking time to do things that were satisfying left her in a state of depression. Depression can be a double-edged sword because it makes everything in our lives feel worse than it may actually be. Ulrich Schimmack, a psychologist at the University of Toronto, says that depression and positive emotions or cheerfulness are traits that greatly influence life satisfaction. Overcoming depression and improving your outlook on life might make the difference between discontentment and fulfillment. In fact, depression is a more important factor in determining your outlook on life than anxiety or anger. Depression is such a powerful force that it can even override the positive benefits of being active or social. Professor Schimmack says, "Likewise, positive emotions and cheerfulness carried more weight than other upbeat traits in most surveys." The results were similar for men and women. "The strong influence of depression rather than anxiety and vulnerability suggests that a lack of meaning is more detrimental to life satisfaction than stress and worries."[27]

Sometimes depression is a temporary state caused by our own fear. It can be fear of letting go of old ideas or old habits—things that keep us from moving forward in our maturity. In these cases, our awareness of depression should give us the impetus to let go and move on. Carol was smart to recognize that she needed to start saying yes to new activities to overcome her depression.

SIMPLICITY MADE SIMPLE

Today is a good day to take some time to rediscover the simplicity of doing something that satisfies you. Here are some thoughts to help you get started:

EVALUATE YOUR OWN LEVEL OF LIFE SATISFACTION. Ask yourself questions such as: As I have grown older, do things seem better or worse than I thought they would be? Have I been given more breaks in life than most people? Am I happier now, or do I think life is simply dreary at this age? Was I happier when I was younger? Perhaps you think these are the best years of your life or better yet, you believe that there are still lots of new and exciting things in store for the future. If you are optimistic and continue to find life interesting, you are probably satisfied. However, if you find life boring and monotonous, and simply feel tired and old, then it's time to get yourself moving and doing more interesting and satisfying activities.

Author Jean-Louis Servan-Schreiber suggests in his book, *The Art of Time*,[28] that we substitute the word *life* instead of *time* in the following phrases to **GAIN THE RIGHT PERSPECTIVE:**

➤ No *time* for

➤ I don't have the *time*

➤ Using my *time* well

➤ Losing *time*

➤ I'm going to spend some *time* on it

➤ Mastering my *time*

When we make that one-word substitution, we realize that time and life are in fact the same thing. This should be enough motivation to make us place the importance on it that it deserves.

FILL YOUR MIND WITH THOUGHTS THAT ARE TRUE, PURE AND LOVELY because things that disturb, spoil, drain, reduce or shorten life are not good things in life. Do your best to avoid a negative attitude, and put on a happy face!

WATCH PEOPLE. People-watching is one of my favorite pastimes—I love to imagine what they are thinking or saying. For example, I can invent an entire life story simply by watching a young couple in the park. If they are holding hands, I assume they are madly in love. If they are not, I wonder if they are angry, arguing, or maybe they are brother and sister? Who knows? It's just fun. Now, imagine what others are thinking about you—when they see you in a public place. Are they imagining a happy person who is satisfied with her life? Or do they feel sad that you appear to be so lonely? The answer is in how you act, look and feel.

Make a list of all the **HOBBIES** or other activities that you have always wanted to try but have never had the time. Now pick just one—and do it this year.

Lord, today I will take time to live well and focus
on what is good, and pure, and lovely. Thank You
for giving me reasons to be cheerful in heart
and satisfied with how I spend my life.

PART FOUR

The Time for Change

CHANGE MAY BE ONE of the most difficult things to embrace about time, but its anticipation is the anchor of our hope. God knew that change would be good for us. We can remain stable through change because God changes not; but in His great source of creative ideas there is something new to discover about Him each day. As we move through the phases of our lives, we will learn, do and teach others what we have enjoyed most. Take time to apply the lessons from this next section of the book and learn to embrace your times of change.

Finding Balance
in Youth

Foolishness is bound in the heart of a child. . . .

—PROVERBS 22:15 (KJV)

Young children are often foolish and do dangerous things simply because they don't know better or understand the consequences of their decisions. As we mature in wisdom and common sense, we learn the difference between right and wrong. We understand that our actions have consequences. Consequences can be good or bad depending on our choices. If we make bad choices, our lives get off balance and we suffer. If we make good choices, our lives have balance and we thrive.

One of the best definitions of a balanced life was written by Christian recording artist Rob Mullins, who said, "Balance is a concept of staying on your feet, in charge of your life, and abreast of conflict while living on earth. In my experience, nothing is more important than balance, and understanding its concept is the key to a healthy life."[29] Obviously, as we go through the different phases and stages of life—the challenges for maintaining balance change. As we go through our life course from birth to death, we will find the experience vastly different at each stage. Most people recognize four fundamental life stages, each lasting about twenty to twenty-two years, and each with a unique social role at each stage. These are childhood, ages zero to twenty; adulthood, twenty-one to forty-one; midlife, ages forty-two to sixty-two; and elderhood, ages sixty-three and up.

THERE IS A TIME TO CHOOSE YOUR LIFE PATH

First, let's examine what adults, ages twenty-one to forty-one, do with their time. These years are critical because the choices we make during this time can affect the rest of our lives. The young, freedom-loving part of this age wants to continue to explore and expand its world. When we are this age, we want to try new things and discover new ideas. We think we can have it all. I know I did. But the other side of this life stage wants to establish roots and settle down. As we begin to feel confident in our own authority and wisdom, we find a struggle against the recklessness of our youth. Resolving this struggle will require honest evaluation and reckoning to accept the fact that we cannot be and do everything we thought we could when we were twenty. We must choose a path that we will follow for at least the next several years.

As we move through this phase of life, we must learn to either adjust our idealistic expectations to reality or be forced to start over again with a new path and plan. These are hard decisions. It is during this stage of life that most marry, raise children, purchase a home and set their career path—all of which are major life decisions that require the giving up of something in order to have something else.

For example, the idea of being a professional ballet dancer doesn't fit too well with the idea of motherhood. It is extremely difficult to live a life on the road and still properly raise a child. Most would conclude that there simply isn't enough time in a day to do both. If we were to try to balance two equally strenuous paths, we would find it difficult to do both well. Most likely, something would suffer for the success of the other.

This time period is the busiest stage of life, especially if we are raising a family. Young children require time—lots of time. But we must remember that this is "just a stage" in our lives. It is only for a season. Enjoy this season. Our children are only young once—we won't want to miss it. This is the stage in which many people begin to feel overwhelmed, stressed and short on time. Ultimately, the only way to reduce the busyness and the stress is to choose our priorities (God, family, service to others). God will accept the fact that we are short on devotion time. He gives us grace for this stage of life—and happily accepts our two-minute prayers each day.

Although God gives us grace for this stage of life—other opportunities may not be so forgiving. If, for example, you are volunteering at the crisis center, teaching Sunday school, heading up the art auction and wondering why you are feeling stressed, the answer is simple—you need to make better choices. Busyness in this stage of life is your own fault.

Your family circle should be served first before you commit to serving outside interests. Being a wife and a mother is a full-time job. There will be plenty of time later in life to head up committees and serve your community.

But if you have young children right now, then the job God has given you is to serve your family.

Guideposts writer Sue Monk Kidd recognized the magnitude of this stage of life one night when her colicky infant daughter awoke for the third time. Just as she had finally rocked her back to sleep, Bob, her three-year-old, woke in desperate need of water. As Mom whispered, "In a little while," little Bob yelled at the top of his lungs, "But I want some water now!" The baby jerked and cranked up her cry—as Mom's own heart raged, "Lord, I know it's Mother's Day, but I don't want to be a mother today. I'm sick of it."

Her husband waded into the shrieking darkness, rubbing his eyes as if he'd wakened into a real live nightmare. "What's going on?" he said. "Here, give the children to me," he said, bravely. "You go to bed."

"They're all yours," Sue said as she thrust daughter Ann into his arms. Sue fell into bed, despising the way she felt. "Oh, Lord, help me," she prayed as she drifted over the edges of sleep. "Help me find some joy again."

On the drive home from church that morning little Bob's voice floated over the front seat. "We talked about mothers in Sunday school. My teacher said I made you a mother when I was borned. Tell me the story of when I was borned—I mean born."

Reluctantly, Sue began, "It was late one night and Daddy and I had waited and waited for you. We thought you never would get here. But finally you decided to come. Daddy drove me to the hospital."

"Then I was born?" he said, urging Mom to continue. "Did you hold me?"

"Yes, we had a long visit that night. You were wrapped in a blanket." Then Sue's memory stirred, "I nearly forgot there was a card tucked in your blanket that night, a card from the hospital."

"What did it say?" Bob asked.

Sue found the card in the baby book; across the front it was personalized with a slightly faded, slightly smudged inkblot of his hand, five newly born fingers and one incredibly tiny palm. A simple greeting card verse read:

> "Make the most of every day
> For time does not stand still.
> One day this hand will wave good-bye
> While crossing life's brave hill."[30]

For Sue Monk Kidd, this simple verse was a picture of how precious and fleeting each moment with a child really is. As all of us that are beyond the "mommy stage" of life realize, God knew what He was doing when He created motherhood for those that are young.

SIMPLICITY MADE SIMPLE

As you journey through this stage of life, here are some thoughts to help:

BE TRUE TO YOUR PERSONAL PRIORITIES for this time of life. Simply focus on being a wife and a mother, and on the spiritual aspect of your life.

Sit down three or four times a year to **REEVALUATE YOUR ACTIVITIES** in light of your family's ever-changing pace.

BE SENSITIVE TO THE SPIRIT'S LEADING. If God has other activities that He wants you to engage in, then He will bring them to you. Take the time to sit quietly and focus on His will—not your own.

PRUNE BACK the "business" of your life, so that you can thrive. By taking the time to simplify your life, you give yourself the freedom to fully appreciate it. This is the beauty of a balanced life.

BE WARY OF OTHER PEOPLE'S OPINIONS. At this stage of life it is easy to feel insecure and unsure, which will leave you vulnerable to the opinions of others. Choose your counsel wisely and recognize that you will never be able to make everyone happy. For example, the relationships between wives and their mothers-in-law are notoriously fraught with conflict. Everyone means well—but not everyone is good at expressing it. If this is true in your situation, learn to accept the comments of your mother-in-law with grace; simply thank her for her concern and wisdom. Then express your desire to find your own way without alienating her or the relationship of your children to her. This is an important balance that requires patience and grace. God has plenty of extra grace if you just ask Him for it.

> Lord, there are so many wonderful options that
> compete for my time. Please help me to keep a clear
> perspective of my priorities and refrain from
> overcommitting in my life. I know that I will remain
> in perfect peace if I am following You.

Midlife Mania

A time to get, and a time to lose;

a time to keep, and a time to cast away.

—ECCLESIASTES 3:6 (KJV)

Each phase of life brings with it the opportunity for new experiences. But sometimes accepting the new requires letting go of the old. Midlife, ages forty-two to sixty-two, is definitely a time to cast away a lot of the old, because there is so much new to look forward to. Unless we are willing to let go and move forward, we will not be able to find balance in this middle stage of life.

Guideposts writer Don Bell wrote of his own letting go experience:

> I've heard it said that when the rodeo gets in a cowboy's bloodstream it never leaves. My youth was spent as a bucking horse rider. I traveled this world over until I quit the rodeos because Uncle Sam needed me in World War II. When I returned to the

states after a long, bloody siege in Europe, I knew my days as a bronc rider were over. Adolf Hitler seemed to have taken my nerves.

But then I heard that the Wolf Point, Montana, rodeo paid big cash prizes. Though I was forty years old and scared, I decided to enter the bronc-riding contest. I rode a big Canadian bronc. But I had a terrible time with him. And as I held on to the bucking horse, I could see in my mind this pick-up rider coming to get me. He wasn't dressed in cowboy garb. This fellow seemed to have a white sheet over him. His face I could not see. Over his shoulder he seemed to carry a scythe. I knew it was Death who wanted to take me off this bucking horse. In my mind, he sat me on the ground safe but I heard a message: Don, you are bucking a young man's game. It's time you quit.

Those words I still hear. They tell me there are some things older folks shouldn't mess around with as we did when we were young.

Sooner or later, there's a time when you've got to let go and say good-bye to outgrown things. Is there an old habit, an outmoded dream, a stubborn attitude, belief or desire you're clinging to? Think a moment. Could this be your time to "cast away"?[31]

Midlife certainly has its discomforts, but as with all life transitions, one can emerge from this experience feeling freer, healthier and more confident. As we learn to let go of outdated ideas, dreams, and schemes, we can embrace the future. It's all a matter of attitude. Those who view this stage of life with only the potential for the negative lose the opportunity for what could be their most productive and fulfilling stage of life. Today, fifty is the new forty—or even thirty. With our life span expected to last until age seventy-five, we may only be at the halfway mark with a lot of living to do. It's exciting to think how we can maintain more productive lives, extended careers, better health, and more opportunities than any other generation before.

EMBRACE YOUR PURPOSE

As women, this is the time when our life experiences bring a dimension that has depth, real value, and substance of heart and soul. Although we will experience significant biological and physical changes during this time of life, we gain the potential for spiritual learning and embracing life to its fullest. Midlife is a time for wholeness, integrity, love, independence, and a time for healing and finding one's true calling.

Spiritually, this will be our most proactive season. Universally, midlife brings with it a caring of the soul. We finally understand the need and are willing to make the time to incorporate our spiritual life into our daily life. We know that our souls require time and reflection. It is only when we become more intimate with our Creator that we can truly know ourselves and find the purpose for our being. We find new meaning and appreciation for life as we connect at a deeper level with our own soul and the will of the Father. We recognize the gift of the Holy Spirit working in our lives, directing us with purpose.

This newfound purpose leads us to discover our true calling. As we realize that our career could last for the next twenty to twenty-five years, we desire to find work that is more satisfying, fulfilling and creative. One friend of mine changed jobs after her teenage daughter's frightening experience with cancer. When her daughter was finally through this difficult passage, Linda examined her own career and decided to make a change. She knew that she wanted to do work that was more significant. She now works for a nonprofit corporation that raises funds for cancer research.

Midlife is also a time of retrospection. As we become more attuned to the inner voice of God speaking to us, we realize our obligation to serve others. Our attitudes and character become focused on meeting the needs of others rather than putting ourselves first. We understand that losing can have honor. We are more cooperative and less competitive. We value honesty and integrity and put more weight in the considered opinions of others. And we dedicate ourselves to prayer and meditation as a regular part of our daily lives.

We also have learned the value of conflict. We understand that as we walk through the conflicts of life we gain inner strength and stronger faith. As we emerge to this new stage of life we may face the pressure of "sandwiched" responsibilities of raising our own teenage children and caring for our parents. But we *can* find balance if we are disciplined.

We know that God will not ask more of us than He will accomplish through us. At this stage of life we have finally realized that it is not of our own doing that we succeed, but it is by the submission of ourselves that God succeeds. It is in the tough times that we often learn perspective. We see that what appeared to be a monumental issue was probably more truthfully our own overdramatization, or at least not nearly as enormous an issue as we originally thought. In other words, we now pick our fights and let go of many lesser conflicts without confrontation. We realize that this middle stage of life will take us to some of our lowest valleys and highest mountains, so we don't let every situation become a crisis. We cope. We cast away. And we trust God.

SIMPLICITY MADE SIMPLE

The journey through the middle stage of life will be exciting, so hang on tightly. Here are some tips for this traveling experience:

BE PATIENT WITH YOURSELF. Best-selling author Gail Sheehy surveyed thousands of women and found that "those with the poorest sense of well-being were, on average, forty-seven years old—the pits—while those enjoying the highest sense of well-being were fifty-three—the peak."[32] It makes perfect sense because the fear and depression of menopause usually makes its mark around forty-seven years of age. But once we get through this rite of passage, we find the blessings of our fifties.

Sheehy also wisely says, "Second Adulthood is not about repeating ourselves; it's about finding a new version of attractiveness. It's making the most of whatever external beauty we have, but also activating sources of internal value and defying the 'beauty myth' that constrained us in the First Adulthood."[33] When we accept the reality of this new phase of beauty, we will finally **ACCEPT OURSELVES AS GOD SEES US**—from the inside out.

"Learn to **DISTINGUISH THE DIFFERENCE BETWEEN PROBLEMS AND INCONVENIENCES**," says Christian speaker and author Elizabeth Cody Newenhuyse.[34] Our burden diminishes when we learn this lesson, and we find humility in the fact that life is not about what we want to accomplish but what God wants to accomplish in and through us. My prayer each day is that God will help me to accomplish all that He wishes me to. And that is very different from asking Him to help me accomplish all that I *think* He wants me to.

BALANCE EQUALS FLEXIBILITY. Psychiatrist M. Scott Peck says, "Balancing is the discipline that gives us flexibility. Extraordinary flexibility is required for successful living in all spheres of activity."[35] As we mature, we realize that our capacity to be flexible in our daily needs, goals, duties and responsibilities is a delicate balance that involves the giving up for the greater good.

BE A MENTOR. As you gain the wisdom of this stage of life, help someone younger than you through her phases. Recently, as I sat chatting with a client, I noticed a look that signaled stress on her face. I have known her for seventeen years and had never seen her look so distressed. As we chatted, she expressed that she was having some physical and emotional issues that were quite disturbing to her. After asking a few leading questions, we both laughed. Her "symptoms" were clearly those of the beginning of menopause. She was having trouble sleeping; she was edgy and forgetful. She thought she was losing her mind and was afraid to even discuss it with her husband. She was encouraged to find out that most women experience these symptoms and that she would recover. I suggested she call her doctor and have a blood test taken to determine where she was in this passage, so they could put together a plan of relief.

> **Father, in Your great scheme of things, You have given me energy before I had wisdom, and wisdom now that I move more slowly. Because You are perfect, I will trust that You have a perfect plan for this time in my life. I will be slow to speak and quick to listen to Your voice.**

Wise Women

"I thought, 'Age should speak;
advanced years should teach wisdom.'"

—JOB 32:7 (NIV)

In order to recognize a great truth, it must be experienced in your life. Job's friend Elihu recognized the truth that God was the only source of real wisdom, but he did not use God's wisdom to help Job. It is unfortunate that Elihu could recognize where wisdom came from but was not willing to seek it or acquire it. To become wise should be a lifelong pursuit. It is not enough to *know about* wisdom; we must make it a part of our daily lives.

This latter stage of life, ages sixty-three to eighty-three, should be our wisest experience. I think that we reach a point where we know that if something appears bad or destructive in our lives, it is usually because we have not yet learned to understand it. Psychologist and author of *Embracing Uncertainty*, Susan Jeffers, says, "How elevating and wise it is to think of 'defeat' as a way to 'shape the soul and let the glory out.'"[36] The point is that the wisdom of age teaches us that we can learn from all of life's situations, good and bad.

NOW IS THE TIME TO ENJOY YOURSELF

Life can be extremely productive after age sixty-five too. Our attitude and how we perceive life at this age can make all the difference. In most cases, we will get what we expect from life. An article in *Psychology Today* titled, "Peaking after 65: Here's How: Performance Doesn't Have to Diminish with Age," quoted Sayra F. Lebenthal, founder and chairperson of Lebenthal & Co., a Manhattan municipal bond dealer, as saying, "I can't imagine anything more important than what I do, why on earth should I want to stop?"[37] At ninety, she still goes to the office five days a week. Lydia Bronte, a gerontologist, says that Lebenthal and others are evidence that performance and creativity don't have to diminish with age, particularly when men and women take care of themselves physically. Certainly, good health is an important factor that makes a big difference in whether or not we will enjoy these latter years. And most of those sixty-five plus who are still active watch their diet and exercise regularly. Nearly all those still working or active in service to others share a passionate love for what they do, along with a positive attitude.

The good news for people approaching this phase of life is that they are likely to live longer, healthier and more independent lives than those of earlier generations. We have learned that the challenges that we thought were a necessary part of the normal aging process are not always inevitable. We may not be able to change our genes, but we can control many factors that shape our health at this age. Simple lifestyle changes such as consistent exercise and a healthy diet can reduce the effects of disease and aging. By taking the time to take care of our bodies, we in turn take care of our minds by giving ourselves the ability to keep them busy and working.

Learning to apply all the wisdom of our years is the key to understanding. Guideposts writer Dorothy Shellenberger wrote about some words of wisdom she found:

> Several years ago, I came across a paraphrased copy of an anonymous prayer written by a nun in the seventeenth century that I read and reread often during the year. If you are like me and have reached that age in your life when time streaks by like a jet at thirty thousand feet, then perhaps you would like to join me in the litany I have borrowed from this lady who lived three hundred years ago and make it your prayer too:
>
> *Lord, Thou knowest better than I know myself that I am growing older and will someday be old. Keep me from the fatal habit of thinking I must say something on every subject and on every occasion.*
>
> *Release me from craving to straighten out everybody's affairs.*
>
> *Make me thoughtful but not moody, helpful but not bossy. With my vast store of wisdom, it seems a pity not to use it all. But Thou knowest Lord that I want a few friends at the end.*
>
> *Keep my mind free from the recital of endless details. Give me wings to get to the point.*
>
> *Seal my lips on my aches and pains. They are increasing— and love of rehearsing them is becoming sweeter as the time goes by.*

I dare not ask for grace enough to enjoy the tales of other's pains, but help me to endure them with patience.

I dare not ask for improved memory but for a growing humility and a lessening cocksureness when my memory seems to clash with the memories of others. Teach me the glorious lesson that occasionally I may be mistaken.

Keep me reasonably sweet. I do not want to be a saint—some of them are so hard to live with. But a sour old person is one of the crowning works of the devil.

Give me the ability to see good things in unexpected places and talents in unexpected people. And give me, Oh Lord, the grace to tell them so.[38]

As we live the years that God ordains, I hope we all will shine with the glory of God's wisdom from within. That for me is the perfect crown for a life well lived. Our goal for this wonderful age should be to maintain a good attitude, live a balanced lifestyle and give priority to the time with God that He deserves. As one anonymous woman in her eighties said about looking back on her life, "One must wait until evening to appreciate the splendor of one's day."

By now we know that life is a series of beginnings and endings. We are more conscious of doing things more deliberately, and, hopefully, have learned to take our time and make the most of living.

SIMPLICITY MADE SIMPLE

Here are a few thoughts to help you chart your way through this part of your life's journey:

ADD MEANING TO YOUR LIFE. If you are willing and able to keep working through these golden years, then consider changing careers and finding work that is more significant to you. Knowing that you are working at something good that serves the needs of others can give your life more meaning. As we work to help improve the quality of others' lives, we help ourselves as well by finding a sense of purpose for our own lives.

PLAN AHEAD. If you are approaching this wonderful phase of life, be sure to plan for it. At least two to five years before you retire, begin talking to your family and friends about your expectations for the years ahead. This will help others adjust to the changes you plan to make and even engage their help in making your plans succeed.

WRITE DOWN YOUR EXPECTATIONS. Be as specific as you can. For example, if you plan to participate in charitable activities, then start investigating your options. If education is an area that interests you, then begin to narrow down your areas of interest. Perhaps like my friend Jan, you would like to focus on traveling to a specific country or simply dedicate yourself to educating Third World children. Then research which organizations are involved in doing this and find out exactly what you can do to help.

Be sure to **TALK WITH YOUR SPOUSE** and consider his expectations as well. Retirement can be a very difficult time for couples, thus putting a lot of stress on the marriage. Experts recommend retiring together if possible because it allows each of you to be empathetic toward the other as you both deal with the same issues.

ORGANIZE YOUR TIME. If you are married, schedule "couples" activities and other social events. Also schedule individual time to maintain your sense of autonomy. If you are single, organizing your time is even more critical. Be sure to plan for social and learning activities.

FIND A PURPOSE. You are more available for God's will now than ever before. Seek out where God is working and join Him.

MAINTAIN YOUR MENTAL AND PHYSICAL WELL-BEING. Some decline in our physical performance is only natural, but moderate exercise, especially in our daily activities, will help maintain the way our bodies function. And if they don't work as well as we'd like, then adopting a sense of humor can help!

MINIMIZE YOUR HEALTH PROBLEMS. By finding out about your own chances of developing conditions such as high blood pressure or diabetes, you can minimize your risk and lessen the effects.

STAY ENGAGED in life and avoid isolation. Maintaining relationships with people is an important component of mental and physical health. Stay involved with your family and friends. Participate in community events, whether you choose to volunteer or simply enjoy leisure activities.

SET GOALS for yourself and work toward them. Exercising, eating nutritiously, getting adequate sleep and keeping a positive attitude are all worthy goals that can greatly improve the quality of your life.

ATTRACT LIKE MINDS. Nonprofit groups tend to attract like-minded people. Choosing to volunteer with a group that has similar interests to yours can make the process simpler and give you the added bonus of an opportunity to make new friends.

> Lord, thank You for this precious gift of life. Help me to recognize this new phase as an opportunity to explore the desires of my heart that I never had time for before. Ignite in me the purpose You have ordained for me to fulfill.

Embracing Change

"Now do not be stiff-necked . . .

but yield yourselves to the Lord. . . ."

—2 CHRONICLES 30:8 (NKJV)

Hezekiah was a king dedicated to God and to the spiritual life of his nation. He urged everyone to return to God. He told them not to be stubborn, but to yield themselves to the Lord. Yielding requires total obedience: submitting our bodies, minds, will and emotions to Him. It is not until we are most pliable to God's will that He can use us. Submitting ourselves requires us to change: to change our plans, our will and to adjust our lives to that which God wills us to do.

It is this very thing—change—that keeps most of us from the good work that God has for us. How often have you prayed for God to show you His will for your life? And then as soon as you feel a nudge that might take you in a direction in which you are not comfortable—do you pull back? That nudge was probably the Holy Spirit attempting to set you on a new course that would have placed you directly in the will of God. But our fear of the unknown, our fear of change and our fear of failure, which keep us from accepting the challenge, are exactly the things that God can use to prove Himself. God never asks us to do something that *He* is not capable of completing in us. The problem is that too often we think God will only ask us to do something that *we* are already capable of doing.

EXPRESS YOUR OBJECTIONS, THEN ENJOY THE RIDE

It's okay to offer objections. It's okay to talk to God and tell Him how incapable you feel. But it is not okay to disobey Him. Moses is a good example of someone who didn't feel qualified for the job God was assigning him. "O my Lord, I am not eloquent, neither before nor since You have spoken to Your servant; but I am slow of speech and slow of tongue" (Exodus 4:10, NKJV). "O my Lord, please send by the hand of whomever else You may send" (Exodus 4:13, NKJV).

Clearly, Moses was afraid of failing. But Moses was obedient and, as a result, God succeeded with His plan through Moses. This change or adjustment that Moses had to make was a direct order from God. Change is inevitable—sometimes change seems sudden as if God intervenes—willing you to take a new course. Other times change takes place practically unnoticed, it simply happens through the natural ever-changing course of life.

What if your body never grew and changed? You could find yourself as an adult in the body of a child—rendering you incapable of implementing the knowledge you gained. We are blessed that God's design perfectly matches our physical ability, even if we don't always agree.

In her book, *God, I Know You're Here Somewhere*, Elizabeth Newenhuyse says, "Even the most easygoing, take-it-as-it-comes types among us probably carry around mental snapshots of 'The Way It's Supposed to Be.' It's constructive to have a sense of who you are and where you're going. But all the plans and designs and lists and goals in the world can't buffet us against life's unpredictabilities."[39] God knew the change was coming and He allowed it. He certainly doesn't want us sitting around and throwing a poor pity-me party. He wants us to get to work.

Perhaps we find change so difficult because it requires us to give up something. We may need to give up our ideas or plans in order to accept the change. For example, as we age, we must give up our definition of youth as beauty. M. Scott Peck says, "Balancing is a discipline precisely because the act of giving up is painful. . . . The only alternative to this giving up is not to travel at all on the journey of life."[40] Sometimes, it's simply giving up the reassurance of something comfortable and familiar—like a job. Even if the job isn't great, we know what it is and that may be enough comfort for us not to look for another. Sue Monk Kidd wrote about her own experience:

> It is late autumn, one of those wind-washed days that scour the trees bare. My daughter Ann and I are raking leaves in the backyard—ten thousand crimson reminders that the seasons of change always come. For weeks now I've resisted a beckoning inside to make some changes in my career, to stretch out toward new horizons and projects I've dreamed of pursuing. It will mean leaving behind beloved work I've done many years, and that . . . well, that's inconceivable. I finish raking and bag the leaves, determined to put the stirrings for change out of my mind once and for all.
>
> "Look, Mama, look at the scuppernong vines!" Ann stands at the back fence, leaning against her rake. The vines, a hearty

muscadine variety familiar to the South, are wild and thick, bare as a skeleton. "Why don't you make your basket?" she says. Not long ago I took a basket-weaving class with some friends and ever since I'd been telling the family I was going to make a basket all on my own.

I clip the vines but find they are practically unweavable, much too stiff to bend. I'm about to give up when I get an idea: Soak the vine. I curl them in a pail of water and sure enough, soon they are soft and pliable. Now I sit among the oaks and weave the vines around a base of sticks, my fingers moving in and out with unbroken rhythm. As the tiny basket unfolds, I cannot help thinking about the strands of my own life, about God who comes at the appointed season wanting to weave new patterns. Deep inside I hear God ask me a question: "Sue, are you pliable enough?"[41]

Unless we are willing to yield our stiff necks to the changes that God wants to bring to our lives, we will miss the opportunity for an intimate relationship with the One who loves us the most.

SIMPLICITY MADE SIMPLE

Here are ways to remain pliable and ready for the next phase of life:

ACCEPT CHALLENGE. Recognize that there will be times when you will be tested emotionally. Look deep within and seek the strength you need from the One above. Let this challenge remind you that living a full life requires the ability to see life from a balanced perspective between the joyful times and the difficult.

Negotiating change can be stressful. But planning for it, and **SEEING CHANGE AS A PROGRESSION OF STEPS**—rather than a monster-sized mountain to climb—will help make the challenge less stressful.

Remember that **YOU ARE NOT ALONE**. Maintain your support group links by phone, e-mail or in person. The most important relationship to maintain is the one with God. Remember to pray and read your Bible regularly and seek comfort in God's promise to be with you always.

Transition times can feel lonely. Author Robert Wicks writes, "When we feel our heart is breaking or the energy for life is slowly draining from us, if we can **SEE BEYOND THE FEELINGS** of loss or alienation, if we can be open to hope, we may experience a softening of our soul, a change of heart, a paradigm shift. And, in that moment, we have an opportunity to experience God and our lives in a new, deeper way."[42]

THE ANSWER TO BOREDOM IS CHANGE! All of us have experienced times when life simply seemed boring. The only real cure for boredom is change, and change requires taking risks. Motivational author Og Mandino says, "Risk taking is a major part of the 'cure' so don't hope that somehow you'll be able to avoid it."[43]

LOSE CONTROL. Living life is like learning to ride a bike; as long as we remain stiff, attempting to control our arms and legs, we will fall. But when we relax and trust gravity, we ride with ease. Control is probably one of the hardest things for us humans to give up. Yet this yielded state is exactly where God, the Master Potter, wants us to be—in His hands—giving Him complete control.

Each of us responds differently to change. Those who best handle change are more flexible and active in their responses. The more rigid or passive we are, the more difficult it will be for us to accept change. It is common to initially resist change by denying it or ignoring our problems. And it's easy to get stuck in the phase and feel trapped. The sooner we are able to **RECOGNIZE THIS SIMPLY AS A PHASE** in the process, the easier it will be for us to move forward toward the active stage of dealing with change.

ACTIVE STRATEGIES FOR COPING include getting support from others; lowering our expectations and taking one step at a time; being flexible in our view of the situation; seeing change as an opportunity to learn new things and grow; learning to see humor in situations (I know from personal experience that God has a great sense of humor); taking care of yourself physically, emotionally and spiritually; journaling or engaging the ear of a supportive friend; and giving yourself time to adjust. It's worth it. Trust God; He knows what He's doing.

Father, I realize You must love change, for Your mercies are new every morning. Your sunsets are never the same, and no two leaves or snowflakes are alike. Help me to embrace the changes You have designed for me to enjoy.

Celebrate!

And the third day there was a marriage in Cana of Galilee;
and the mother of Jesus was there: And both Jesus was
called, and his disciples, to the marriage.

—JOHN 2:1–2 (KJV)

T his verse always fascinated me. Part of me wants to believe that Jesus had
better things to do with his time than to go party at a wedding. On the other
hand, I am grateful for this verse because it makes me stop to think about how
many opportunities for celebration or meaningful interaction I might miss if I
didn't think it was okay to make them a priority over my work. Even Jesus took
time from His work to attend a wedding. Jesus knew how to find balance in His
life—despite all He had to do. In the midst of His mission to save the world, He
took time out to attend a wedding. Why?

The answer is simple. We remember longer the days that were different from
the rest, the times we paused from routine to mark the moment or day as memorable. Holidays, celebrations, the "time-outs" that we took to refresh ourselves

are remembered best. Besides, there is so much to celebrate: our freedom, our God-given talents and the everyday blessings that we enjoy but too often take for granted. Life is special—and we can honor life by celebrating. Celebration can be the best way to encourage learning, living and loving. Celebration always includes people. We learn from being around others and watching how they live life, and we love celebrating and learning to enjoy each other.

When was the last big celebration that you remember? If you have to think back to years ago, it's definitely been too long since you have celebrated! It doesn't have to be expensive or require months of planning. We bring more joy to life when we learn to celebrate simple, ordinary living.

I remember when my great-grandmother died; we found a chest full of things that she had put away, saving them for special occasions. When we found her "good" linen tablecloth, it was worn through at the folds. It was sad to see that she had missed an opportunity for good living. Instead, she lived afraid to use her tablecloth because it might get ruined, and it did—but not from use.

THERE'S ALWAYS A REASON TO CELEBRATE!

Celebration adds intrinsic value to our lives. For our children, it can be the reward for accomplishment: learning to ride a bicycle, learning their ABC's or making the hockey team. If we appreciate and approve of our children's accomplishments with the honor of celebration, we push them along their personal journey with joy. This will encourage them to achieve more, and to seek things of value because *they* feel valued. We can reward them for good moral behavior through celebration as well. As children learn and grow spiritually, we can encourage them to continue to seek and keep God's instructions.

Sometimes, we simply don't think we have the time to celebrate. But it is in just this kind of atmosphere that celebration is most important. Despite life's rapid pace we must take the time to celebrate because it has a universally positive effect on all of us. Celebration reduces the tremendous pressures that confront each of us daily. Simply taking the time to change the atmosphere to a positive one relieves the turmoil and renews the spirit.

Just think how great you felt when you celebrated together as a family for a significant holiday or event. Laughter, fun and the closeness of loved ones gathered together are good for whatever ails us. Celebration is the perfect remedy for those who are discouraged! When we gather together we create and renew relationships. We share, we communicate, and we find ourselves renewed in spirit.

For children, time can seem to move as slow as molasses in January. A mid-month celebration can make the school year pass more quickly. It can give youngsters something to look forward to. Years ago, a friend of mine created color days. One day a month she chose a specific color to celebrate. That day her family dressed in that color, set the table in that color, drew pictures in that color. They even attempted to eat foods the same color. It was quirky, but it became something that her children now continue to do with their own families—I think that says it all. It was creative and memorable, and lots of fun.

The older we get, the faster time seems to move. Celebrations give time a new perspective by marking days as something special rather than allowing our days to run together in a blur. Who says we have to wait for the next wedding (or funeral) to see old Aunt Bess? Heck, half the time I no longer recognize the people at these events because it's been so long since I last saw them. For all I know, I could be at the wrong wedding or funeral and I'd never know it!

Let's learn to celebrate the daily blessings of life. Let's decide today not to wait for the next birthday or wedding or major anniversary. Yes, of course we'll still celebrate the milestones, but let's start celebrating the pebbles too! Go ahead and order one of those flaming flambé desserts, and share it with your grandchildren simply because it's Thursday night. Invite your neighbors—even those you don't know—and make up a batch of hot apple cider and chocolate cookies to celebrate the month of October with them.

Clearly, we need to take the time to rethink some of our priorities and put our lives in better balance with more celebration.

SIMPLICITY MADE SIMPLE

Use these suggestions to get your party plans going:

CELEBRATE AND REMEMBER. My great-aunt Annie was terrific at celebrating life. For no reason at all, she would invite us all out to her farm. One of the greatest gifts she ever gave was the audio gift of remembrance. She had secretly been recording our family get-togethers for years. Then, after several decades, she created a compilation tape and made copies for each of us. The tapes arrived unannounced; what fun it was as we each began to play them. Hearing voices of loved ones long gone, along with our own "young" voices, was a delight to our ears. It brought back memories filled with laughter, tears and love. What a beautiful blessing it was.

TAKE PHOTOS. Today, it's easier than ever to share photo memories, either by e-mail or snail mail. Photos make our gatherings special as we look back and identify those who participated in them; we remember the joy of being together. The photos help us maintain a connection to those who are important in our lives, even if we cannot be with them all the time.

CREATE PRICELESS TRADITIONS. Just as my friend did by creating "color days," you too can create new and precious traditions that can be handed down to future generations. It only takes a little imagination.

CELEBRATE THE SEASONS. I hate snow, but throwing a snow party can make it fun. When we get hit with a big snowstorm, everyone knows that we have the best hill in town for sledding. Our yard fills with children and adults alike, creating a symphony of shrieking voices as they fly down our hill. My friends also know that I hate to shovel snow, so they bless me with a little impromptu party as they gather in my drive to shovel me out! I make hot chocolate and we make sure everyone in the neighborhood has a clear way out.

SEND CARDS FOR NO REASON AT ALL. In this day of electronic communication, receiving a letter or card in the mail is a real treat. Make it a habit to buy a card a month and send it to someone you care about. You will be amazed at the difference it will make in their day.

CELEBRATE AT WORK. Recently, my boss at QVC surprised me with a gorgeous fall bouquet of flowers. It was in celebration of my one-year anniversary. As I sit here enjoying it, I am overwhelmed with the gesture. There are thousands and thousands of people working at QVC, but this bouquet made me feel so appreciated and special. Imagine the difference you can make by extending a simple gesture toward someone with whom you work.

CELEBRATE NEW SPIRITUAL BIRTH. As Christians, the day we were reborn or confirmed in our church is a very special occasion. Why not mark this significance in the lives of your children or grandchildren by throwing a party? It's the perfect way to show them how important their spiritual life is. And it also helps them develop a good perspective for the challenges of this life by reminding them that they have a Father in Heaven Who cares for them.

> Lord, each new day offers a reason to celebrate.
> I will learn to celebrate something each day in honor
> of Your awesome creativity. I will choose to love life
> and rejoice in its gift of time.

Times of Mourning

Blessed are they that mourn:

for they shall be comforted.

—MATTHEW 5:4 (KJV)

When I was a child, I memorized the Beatitudes. I also learned that they were not a multiple-choice list from which I could choose to apply to my life. They must be taken as a whole, yet each beatitude brings a unique blessing. They don't promise us pleasure, laughter or even earthly prosperity, but they do promise us a hope and joy at the deepest level that is independent of our circumstances.

It may seem strange to expect blessings if we grieve, but this is one of the promises that the Lord made to us. There are many different reasons why we mourn. It can be the loss of a spouse, a marriage, a job, a friend, a pet or any other event that leads to crisis. It is the crisis that brings on the mourning. As the verse above tells us, we will have times of mourning but we can be blessed through the process.

I truly grieved when I went through my divorce after twenty years of marriage. A friend literally led me into counseling, which I desperately needed. Through that process I found a book titled *Rebuilding*, by Bruce Fisher, EdD, and Robert E. Alberti, PhD, that I believe is one of the best studies ever written on the grieving process.[44]

Early in the book Dr. Fisher says that if you are at the stage where all you can do is cry, then close the book and cry. At that moment that is exactly where I was, and cry I did. Yet many find crying hard or feel that it shows weakness. God created our tear ducts and He gave us the sensitivity to feel grief; He certainly expects us to cry.

THERE IS A TIME TO CRY

The right formula for beginning the grief process is Tear ducts + pain = tears. Tears bring cleansing and healing. And although you may feel like you will never be able to stop the tears once they start—trust me—you will stop eventually. When I finally stopped crying, I was so dehydrated that my skin was dry and parched like a desert. But it too healed with time (and lots of moisturizer).

Although each of us will grieve differently, we will eventually go through all the same steps of grief, though not necessarily in the same order. Dr. Fisher says there are nineteen steps to the process of losing a spouse, but these steps apply to most losses. They are: Denial, Fear, Adaptation, Loneliness, Friendship, Guilt/Rejection, Grief, Anger, Letting Go, Self-Worth, Transition, Openness, Love, Trust, Relatedness, Sexuality, Singleness, Purpose and Freedom. The climb through these steps is painful, but it can also be a source of our greatest growing and benefit. A time of mourning can be one of the most intimate times in our relationship with the Lord, if we rely on Him through it.

You may think you can simply avoid the process of grieving but you can't—you can only postpone it. Eventually, it will catch up with you. If, for example, you still have unresolved grief from earlier times in your life, you may find it even more difficult to deal with a new mourning crisis. As the present loss activates feelings from the past, it makes resolution difficult. Unless we free ourselves from past losses, we will not be able to work through the new ones.

One friend of mine never mourned through her divorce. Years later, she found herself struggling in all her relationships; as each ended and the losses piled on the old ones, she realized that she never resolved the issues from losing her first marriage. Finally, she got help from a good counselor and faced the pain she thought she could avoid.

The reason we sometimes fight mourning is because the first steps are the most painful. It takes hard work to face them and process the pain. But it's this simple: Unless you take the time to mourn the losses when they happen, it will take a lot more time and energy to deal with them later.

Unfortunately, society can make it hard for us to mourn. Well-meaning friends tell us to get on with our lives, keep ourselves busy and just accept reality. In most cases, these well-meaning folks have not experienced mourning in their own lives. They simply don't realize that their recommendations are not healthy or effective for the process.

We must give ourselves permission to mourn. Like the Beatitudes, we can't pick and choose which blessings we want or which part of the mourning process we will go through. Mourning is a part of the whole picture of our lives. We have to experience each step in order to complete the process. Guideposts writer Roberta Messner wrote about a young man she knew who needed permission to grieve a loss:

> Not a Memorial Day goes by that I don't pause to remember Jim, a Vietnam veteran with post-traumatic stress disorder and depression. Jim served two tours of duty in Vietnam when he was in his late teens, but it was the memory of one particularly horrible night in Southeast Asia that refused to let his mind rest. His best buddy Frank was shot in the chest and bled to death in his arms, despite all Jim's efforts to save his life.
>
> "I haven't been able to enjoy a single moment since then," Jim told me, his vacant eyes fixed on the gray linoleum floor. "What's there to celebrate? Christmas, Easter, my birthday . . . they're all just another day to me." Another day filled with intrusive thoughts, reliving Frank's death in agonizing detail. Another night filled with the dreams of a soldier who blamed himself for his best friend's death.
>
> But then a meeting with Frank's mother changed everything for Jim. "Frank's daddy and I loved him better than anything in the whole world," she told him. "But we knew he would want us to move on with our lives, not spend the rest of our days on might-have-beens. We've released him to the good Lord, Jim, and, oh, how he'd want you to do the same!"
>
> That chance encounter set Jim on the road to a freedom he hadn't known since Vietnam. That day, Jim began to ask God to help him forgive himself for Frank's death. Eventually he

was able to let go of the survivor guilt that had held him in bondage for nearly thirty years.

It was a great gift to be able to watch Jim begin to celebrate life again. And as I did, I said a prayer of thanksgiving for Jim and Frank to the One whose victory makes us truly free.[45]

This story perfectly illustrates how it is possible to get caught on one of the steps in the mourning process. Jim was stuck on the *guilt* step for nearly thirty years. When he finally worked through it he was blessed with a freedom from his pain over the loss of his best friend.

SIMPLICITY MADE SIMPLE

Here are a few ways to embrace the blessings that result from times of grief:

CREATE A COMFORT ZONE. When I was going through my divorce, I spent most of my crying time in a big overstuffed chair with a blanket wrapped around me. I nearly wore out both my blanket and my Bible as I progressed through my mourning.

TALK TO GOD—or scream and yell—whatever it takes to express yourself to your Creator. He will understand and bring you comfort.

ASK FOR HUGS. This is especially necessary if you are mourning the loss of a spouse. Hugs and the comforting touch from friends is critical to helping you heal. At times, I wished someone would simply just hold me. I expected friends to read my mind, but they couldn't. So I've learned to simply ask for a hug whenever I need it. Practice doing the same; your friends will gladly supply all the hugs you need.

LET ANGER BE YOUR FRIEND. Too often we feel that we shouldn't allow ourselves to get angry, thinking that anger is unbecoming or simply not right. The reality is that anger is your friend in the mourning process; it helps you move from the place of denial, fear and loneliness to a place of emotional distance, which is an important step forward. In fact, many of us may never have been this angry before.

GIVE YOURSELF TIME TO MOURN. Most experts agree that the mourning process for any loss is about one year. But for a few, it can take as long as five years.

BUILD A NETWORK OF SUPPORT. Even if you have always been the caregiver or the independent person who is determined to never ask for help, this is the one time you need to ask for help. Some of the best support people are those who are *not* your friends and family, but people who have already walked through the same mourning you are in. Make a list of all your needs and look for help in meeting them. If you need help in getting financial paperwork in order, then enlist an expert to help. If you have unfinished projects in your home, you may need a handyman to take care of repairs.

BE SYMPATHETIC TOWARD YOURSELF. Know that this will be a time of emotional ups and downs. Be aware of your emotional state and don't make important decisions when you're feeling low. Whenever possible, delay decisions with long-term impact until you are on an even keel.

STRENGTHEN YOUR FAITH. Spend time each day in prayer, meditation and reading. Seek help from a spiritual adviser. If you have lost a spouse, you may not feel comfortable in your old church. This is especially true for those going through divorce. That's okay. There are many churches that happily accept people of divorce and offer support classes too. Your faith is important to your well-being. God wants to help you grow to your fullest potential. He can use this crisis to do exactly that. Take this time to learn to adjust and make it a spiritual process of growth as well.

Lord, starting over is difficult, but the alternative
is worse. I do not want to remain unchanged,
or unaware of the new experiences You have
prepared for me today. I will enjoy my time with You,
and I am comforted in knowing that Your
unchanging grace is ready to lift me again.

PART FIVE

The Gift of Time

THERE'S NO GREATER USE of our time than the time we spend seeking God,

listening to His voice, and doing whatever He speaks to our hearts to do.

Time is a gift, but we may find that life becomes filled with interruptions

that could have been avoided if we had planned our day with Him. We will

enjoy time more if we use our unique, God-given spiritual gifts to bless

others. And we can miss the greatest joy of time if we don't rid ourselves

of offenses and receive the new heart that God is ready to give to us.

Time for God

And thou shalt love the Lord thy God with all thy heart,
and with all thy soul, and with all thy mind, and with all
thy strength; this is the first commandment.

—MARK 12:30 (KJV)

What does it mean to completely love God? Obviously, it is important because Jesus says that loving God is the *first* commandment—at the top of the list—the thing we should do before anything else. Clearly, we are commanded to love our Lord with all we are: heart, soul, mind and body (strength). That sounds like a priority to me. How about you? Loving God should be our highest priority in life.

How does your day usually start? My routine is pretty simple. My cat, Miss Peony, climbs on my chest every morning, bats me in the face with her paw and demands to be fed. Her relentless meowing always wins. She dictates that my first step in the morning be to feed her and her brother Percy. Then I start the coffee, take my vitamins, make oatmeal and finally sit down with my Bible. This time at the table belongs to the Lord. This has been my routine for several years. However, it's amazing how simple it is for me to get off track. If I accidentally leave a magazine or newspaper on the kitchen table, guess what happens? Of course, I pick up the magazine or newspaper instead of my Bible.

Why does this happen? I am weak. It doesn't take much to distract me—sad but true. I am a visual person. If it's in front of me, it gets my attention and hence the reason I keep my Bible on the kitchen table at all times. It is my visual reminder. One friend of mine stopped getting the morning newspaper because it was such a distraction for her. The only way she could be assured that she would maintain her quiet time with God in the morning was to eliminate the temptation of the newspaper.

God knows we are weak. That is probably why He loved us first. If He sat around waiting for us to make the first move, He would probably still be waiting. Now He is simply waiting for us to respond. By giving God time we make Him a priority in our lives. Think about all the other things that are priorities in your life: family, church, friends, job, even pets. How much time do you give to each of them every week? Do you designate a specific day to each one? No, of course not. You probably spend time with each of them every day. The same should be true for time spent with God.

Just imagine how God feels. He is ready to fellowship with me at my kitchen table every morning where He faithfully waits for me to show up. What happens when I don't? Just like a family member or friend would feel, I'm sure He is disappointed when I don't take time to hear what He has to say to me.

If you made a date for lunch with friends and then never showed up, never called and never sent a note explaining why you didn't come, they would be hurt. God must feel the same way too: ignored, unimportant and unloved. God wants to hear from you every day—not just on Sunday.

BE AWARE OF GOD'S CONTINUAL PRESENCE

Christians are to worship God all the time. It is not something that we simply relegate to Sunday mornings. As we submit our lives to Him, we worship. Romans 12:1 (NIV) says, "Therefore, I urge you, brothers, in view of God's mercy, to offer your bodies as living sacrifices, holy and pleasing to God— this is your spiritual act of worship." But submission (offering ourselves) can be difficult. Yet we are encouraged to persevere, even when we are discouraged and especially when we are hurting because only God can love us in a way that meets all our needs. Unless we spend time in His arms, we will never find the fulfillment that we are looking for.

Colossians 1:16 (KJV) says, "All things were created by him, and for him." As this verse says, absolutely everything started with God. He *created* us for His purpose. Author of *The Purpose-Driven Life*, Rick Warren, wrote, "Not only is He the starting point for our lives, He is the source of it."[46] So it only makes sense that we would want to spend time with the One who knows us best. Only He knows what is best for us, and how we are best used for His purpose. Yet, many of us spend far more time looking for the answers to our questions with everyone else. Or worse yet, we think we already know the right answers.

In the meantime, the Expert is waiting right at our side—all we have to do is to simply ask Him for guidance. Yet, we go through our lives drawing on our own ideas and our past experiences, or simply do things the way they have always been done before. Then we blame God when things don't work out the way we had hoped. That's when we finally turn to Him, but even then, our prayers are childish: "God, please intervene—make things different. Yes, I know I didn't ask for Your direction, but can You make it right anyhow?"

If only we had taken the time to ask for His guidance from the beginning, we wouldn't find ourselves in such complicated situations. Besides, just think how much spare time we would have if we handed our problems over to Him in the first place.

God loves us. He wants to have an intimate relationship with us. He wants to guide us and bless us with the best. But unless we spend time cultivating a relationship with Him, we will miss out on enjoying the peace His presence offers. It is simple. If we want to know the will of God and hear His voice, we must spend time with Him. It is the only way we will learn to recognize the sound of His voice.

How many times have you asked your spouse to spend more time with you? For most women, it is something we cherish. We don't need expensive gifts or lavish lifestyles; we simply want to know that our husbands think we are a priority in their lives—and that translates into time spent together.

SIMPLICITY MADE SIMPLE

Here are some suggestions to inspire you to create time alone with God:

CHERISH LETTERS FROM HOME. Guideposts writer Isabel Wolseley relates how mid-afternoon is the most important part of the day at her house. That's when the postal truck arrives to drop off the mail. She quickly shuffles through magazines, papers, ads and circulars, looking for personal letters from family and friends. Treasured letters deserve to be savored and served with a cup of tea, a cookie, a footstool and an easy chair. After all, she is holding an author's original, limited edition, signed and dated too, written just for her. But these aren't the only letters that interest Isabel. She also reads some written long ago by men named Paul, John, Peter, James and Jude. "Epistles," the Scriptures call them. These letters bring news of home, where Jesus is waiting to welcome all who love Him along with practical advice on making life more abundant.[47]

PREPARE FOR WORSHIP. Author Barbara Hughes wrote, "God-centered worship starts with focusing on the awesome revelation of God."[48] Just thinking about how awesome God is can be humbling. He is holy; He is omniscient (knowing all). He knows our thoughts before we think them. As we bring this visual picture of God before us, we cannot help but ask how should we worship Him? It is by the conduct of our lives that we bring glory to God. Worship starts with our hearts. It is not an external activity. The more we know God, the more we can love Him. The more we love Him, the more spontaneous our worship can be. Take time to quiet your mind and focus simply on His great love.

PRAY. It's so simple, yet we can find it so difficult. As we grow and learn to know our Lord more, our conversations with Him will come easier. If you are struggling, simply follow the advice of Jesus and start with the Lord's Prayer (Matthew 6:9–13). It's a sure bet.

The Bible says we are to have no other gods before Him. With our busy lives, we don't realize how many idols we place before God; work, family, even church commitments can make God take a back seat. But we have a choice. The truth is that the only choice that lasts forever is God. So make time to **GET YOUR FOCUS CLEAR** and as you do so, challenge whatever priorities you have within you so that God becomes number one. That is the only way to have no other gods before Him.

Worship is not a performance. God says you can serve Him quietly in the privacy of your own home. God does not require elaborate ritual in order to approach Him—He's not about "showy stuff." But you can be so intent on some activity that you neglect the most important thing—simply **ACKNOWLEDGING HIS PRESENCE**. You can also worship God by adopting a right attitude toward others, thus fulfilling the second most important commandment, which is to love your neighbor as yourself (Mark 12:31). What is your attitude toward your neighbors, friends, children and husband? If your attitude is one of love, like the love you receive from God, then you are showing God's love to them. And this is the best kind of worship you can honor Him with.

CHOOSE A SPECIFIC TIME OF DAY to devote to your relationship with God. As with all routines and habits, it is best to establish a set time to spend with Him. I am a morning person, so it just makes sense for my time with God to take place first thing in the morning. Look at your own personality and schedule and decide what time of day is best for you. Then mark it on your calendar and keep this appointment no matter what!

> Lord, as your psalmist David wrote, "In the morning . . .
> you hear my voice; in the morning I lay my requests
> before you and wait in expectation." I will meditate on
> Your ways throughout the day, and "On my bed I
> remember you; I think of you through the watches of the
> night. Because you are my help."[49]

Handling Life's Interruptions

But the crowds learned about it and followed him.
He welcomed them and spoke to them about the kingdom
of God, and healed those who needed healing.

—LUKE 9:11 (NIV)

J esus had tried to slip away quietly from the crowds, but they found him. Instead of showing impatience, He welcomed the people and ministered to their needs. This verse tells us of just one time that Jesus was interrupted, but His life was continuously interrupted and His response was one of loving-kindness and readiness to meet the needs of those who interrupted Him.

How do you respond when you are interrupted? If you are like most of us, you get impatient and consider the interruption a big nuisance. Yet, if we are honest, I am sure we can identify plenty of times that an interruption, in fact, had a positive effect on our lives. Just today I received an e-mail from my friend Deb. A year ago she felt led to make a career change. It was hard because she really loved her job in publishing. Now a year later, even as all is going well with the new job, she was keeping her options open in the publishing world, just in case.

Then Deb's computer crashed—no, it died. Even computer experts couldn't recover her information; her machine wore out completely and nothing could be retrieved. Her old life was gone, every contact, every word—gone. This is what she said, "And having lost my e-mail files I'm now totally removed from my former editing world. I have to wonder if God did that on purpose. I still sometimes ask Him how come I had to leave publishing, and now I know without a doubt that to be obedient to Him I had to leave." What started out as an agonizing computer problem has turned into absolute assurance that she is in God's will. How cool is that?

I was blessed with my assistant Patty as a result of a life interruption also. Patty had recently changed jobs to work for a family-owned retail firm. They are well established in the community and it seemed like a smart and sensible job for her to take. Within five months, she was told the store was closing. She had barely completed her training. What was she supposed to do now? Well, as God would plan it, I needed to hire an assistant at that very time. If Patty had not lost her job she would not have been available to work with me. Patty knows that she need not worry about the future. As long as she follows God's leading and is willing to adapt, she knows all will be well.

Both of these examples illustrate how unwelcome interruptions sometimes bring surprising benefits. Sometimes, an interruption is simply God asking us to pause and reconsider our options. Other times, it may be God's way of offering us new opportunities. Like Deb, in the scheme of God's plans for her life, there must be something that she needs to learn that she could not learn in her old career. Did God *make* her computer crash? No, destructiveness is not in His character. But He is able to turn everything to good that happens to us. God will use this interruption to lead Deb to a place where she can learn new things.

MAKE THE MOST OF LIFE'S TRAFFIC JAMS

Sometimes, life's interruptions are for the benefit of others. An unscheduled event may be an opportunity to give help and encouragement to others, or allow for the possibility of sharing our faith with someone who desperately needs it.

Then again, some interruptions are simply that—interruptions. They may, in fact, be a diversion to keep us from what God does want us to do. In that case, we must learn to deal with them quickly and get back to the task at hand and not attempt to find a spiritual message in every interruption. So how do we know which is which? The short answer is to pray.

Christ certainly prayed about some of the interruptions He experienced. For example, His disciples once came to Him to tell Him that many people from Capernaum, the town they were visiting, were looking for Him. Yet He chose to turn away from this opportunity and travel to another town instead. Mark gives us an important clue, in noting that Jesus was praying when the disciples approached Him (Mark 1:35–39). Perhaps during His prayer time Jesus was led to move on to another town. If so, then clearly the local crowd would have been a diversion from the work God had already declared for Him.

Jeanne Hill, an everyday person commuting home from work, writes about how we can use some of these diversions for the good of many:

> As I was driving home one spring rush-hour, the Phoenix traffic snarled to a halt. Soon cars were honking and drivers were shouting at one another. Some of us just sat with scowling faces. All except the driver on my right.
>
> That driver smiled warmly at me, nodding a greeting. I called across to her, half jokingly, "What's your secret for staying serene in such a traffic jam?"

"Prayer. I use this as a prayer wheel," she said, pointing to her steering wheel. Then she explained how, as she fingered each ridge on her steering wheel, she prayed for someone.

The very next time I got into a traffic jam I tried doing what that friendly driver had done. How quickly a brief prayer for a friend, relative or neighbor popped into mind each time I fingered a ridge on my steering wheel. The second time around my prayer wheel, I added a prayer for the driver in front of me, the one in back of me, and those to my right and left. Soon I'd prayed for all the drivers in view.

When traffic started moving again, I found that not only had the tension from driving eased, but I was a more courteous driver. How could I be otherwise? Praying for my fellow drivers had given me an extra measure of concern for them.[50]

After reading that story, it's going to be hard to justify getting all riled up the next time traffic grinds to a halt, isn't it? Ultimately, it comes down to changing the way we think about interruptions. Especially when we consider that such interruptions may indeed be an encounter with the unseen hand of God.

SIMPLICITY MADE SIMPLE

Here are some tips on how to prepare for life's interruptions:

Take steps daily to **DETERMINE WHEN AN INTERRUPTION IS FROM GOD**, or only a diversion to get you off track. A good approach is to start first by simply praying and asking God to guide you. If the interruption doesn't require immediate attention, then ask God to lead you and give you a sense of what to do. Praying won't guarantee that you won't make any mistakes. But in time, your confidence will increase about the choices you are to make. As you become more alert and sensitive to the Spirit's nudging, the likelihood of choosing the right response will improve too. If you commit daily to prayer regarding your various priorities, eventually, your judgment about interruptions will reach the point where you will recognize the ones that truly need your attention.

SOMETIMES THE ANSWER IS OBVIOUS. If you are interrupted with an emergency that requires hands-on attention, then clear your schedule and get moving.

BE OPTIMISTIC. It's easy to see every interruption as a setback. Instead, ask God to simply increase your optimism regarding interruptions. As you learn to see them as positive possibilities in your life, you will gain blessings you might otherwise have missed. See interruptions as God Himself knocking at your door—wanting you to take a different path than the one you *thought* you were supposed to take.

REFLECT ON THE SCRIPTURES. The Scriptures are full of examples of people who were intentionally interrupted by God: Noah, Saul and all of the disciples, just to name a few. Learn to reflect often on these examples and the lives of those around you. In the end, you will probably find welcome results more often than not.

BE READY AND WILLING TO RESPOND. Pastor Todd Bailey gave a challenge to a congregation: "Will you allow God to interrupt your life?" He went on to say that even if you have been a Christian for years and living a godly life, but seem to be in a rut doing the same thing day in and day out, then perhaps it's time to let God interrupt your life and make changes from just living day to day to living each day ready for an encounter with God.[51] Abraham had an encounter with God when he was seventy-five years old. God told him to leave his country. At one hundred years old, Abraham became a father not only to his son Isaac, but also to many nations. Imagine what Abraham would have missed if he had instead seen this encounter as an unwelcome interruption.

> Father, more than anything else, I want to follow You.
> Thank You for promising to make my way straight.
> I will put my trust in You when life's interruptions
> happen today. Please make clear which way I am
> to go when obstacles fall in my path.

Time to Serve

For we are God's workmanship,

created in Christ Jesus to do good works,

which God prepared in advance for us to do.

—EPHESIANS 2:10 (NIV)

The Bible says in Ephesians 2:9 that we are not saved by doing good deeds, yet verse 10 makes it clear that we were *created* for good works. It is through Christ's sacrifice and the gift of grace that we become Christians. However, our gratitude for this free gift should motivate us to help and serve others with kindness, charity and goodness. We were not saved merely for our own benefit, but as members of the church we are to serve Him and help build up the church. Christ paints a living example of good works with His own life. Good deeds were a way of life for Him and should also be for us.

One of the familiar realities for many churches is that a few people do most of the work. It's that same handful of people that show up for choir practice, work as ushers, teach the children's Sunday school class, etc. Too many people treat church simply as a spectator's sport. They show up and expect everything to run smoothly. As with all things, there should be a balance of workers and watchers, but accomplishing that is easier said than done.

I have been on both sides of this seesaw. I was a member of the same church for twelve years. There I was part of an amazing celebration arts team. On the team we had a music pastor, choreographer, make-up artist, seamstress, orchestral director, set designer and builders, a drama director (me), and a group of nearly one hundred willing participants that worked together to present two full-length musicals each year. It was quite an experience to witness what God did through this group of volunteers. As an outreach ministry, we attracted nearly two thousand attendees for each series of performances. None of us could imagine our lives without being involved in this ministry. But it happened . . . slowly. The music pastor felt called to leave for a church in Tennessee. Soon, one by one, circumstances changed within the church leadership and our individual lives.

Now, many of us have moved to a new and much larger church. This new church doesn't allow new members to participate in ministry for at least one year. I think this is a good rule, but it left us all sitting on the sidelines, so to speak. It felt weird at first. But now, most of us realize that this is our season of rest. That if and when God is ready to give us a new ministry assignment, He will make it clear.

CHURCH IS NOT A SPECTATOR SPORT

Often we talk about our personal lives and our church lives as if they can be separated. The truth is, like the soap opera says, we only have one life to live. Our total well-being is dependent on finding a balance between personal time, family time, work and church. Things usually get out of balance when we lose the focus of our mission or purpose.

The Bible says God directs the lives of his creatures; everyone's life is in His power (Romans 12:2). Unless we know God's purpose for our lives, we will not know how we should focus our lives. We won't know where we should be working.

Motivation is another factor that influences us in our church work. Some folks volunteer because it makes them feel good or worthy. Others volunteer because they are lonely, while others do it simply out of duty—because they feel that they have to do it. Yet, the true motivation should come from our love for God and a desire to please Him, not others. No matter how good our deeds, it's what's in our hearts that matters most to God.

When teaching a seminar on spiritual gifts, our pastor quoted Guideposts writer Shirley Pope Waite who said, "At a football game, eighty thousand people who desperately need exercise come to watch twenty-two players who desperately need rest."[52] Then he brought the analogy closer to home. Pointing out that God gives each of us a gift we are to use in the body of Christ, he went on, "Many folks also look upon church as a spectator sport. They consider themselves to be the audience, with the pastor and choir as actors."

I laughed and yet I wondered, *Does my spiritual life consist only of church services and reading devotional books? Do I allow others to do the work, then reap the benefits? What are gifts I can offer the body of Christ?* The Bible mentions several spiritual gifts that God distributes to His people, including serving, giving, acts of mercy and even practicing hospitality. (For other gifts, see Romans 12:6–8, 1 Corinthians 12:28 and Ephesians 4:11.)

After the seminar, I became aware that God had given me the gift of teaching. I also knew that a gift serves no purpose wrapped up on the shelf. I have now taught a short-term Sunday school class, a Bible study in my home and a class at my community college. I've enjoyed each one!

Where are you in the picture of your church? Are you watching while a few wear themselves out? Or are you feeling worn and tattered? You can find a balance by simply taking the time to step back and take a look around. If you are going at a frantic pace, then it's time to let some things go. You have to take time to nourish yourself or you will not be good in your ministry. By contrast, if you've been going to church just to be served, then you need to find a way to start serving. Church should be about two active reasons, serving and being served. If you don't have both in your life, then you are missing something. They sustain each other—that is the balance.

If you're not sure of your spiritual gift, simply ask God to reveal it to you right now. Your gift may be in knowing just the right words of comfort for a needy soul, or the caring way you prepare a satisfying meal. Once you recognize your spiritual gifts, use them in your home, place of work or school, and within the body of Christ. Remember, you were created for good works. As you enjoy fulfilling your purpose, you will find it is time well spent.

SIMPLICITY MADE SIMPLE

Here are some helpful ways to balance your time for service to the Lord:

GET LEVEL. I once read a story about a pastor's wife whose husband gave her a level to keep on her desk as a reminder to not get off balance. Each time she looked at the level, she was reminded to ask herself about the level of busyness in her life. If the bubble was leaning a little too much to either side, she knew something had to change. Perhaps, we each could use a level for our desks?

Take time to **EVALUATE YOUR PERSONAL SITUATION**. If you have been serving in the same position for what seems like forever and have lost the heart for the work, perhaps God has other plans for you. Pray earnestly for His guidance. If God is in our work, then the work should flow easily and profit others. If instead we have become lifeless and drained and the joy is no longer in it, then it's time to give the job to someone new who can pump some freshness into it.

Recognize that the church is not a building or a location; the members *are* the church. Wherever we are, we are in fellowship with one another. As members, we have an obligation to **SERVE ONE ANOTHER WITH OUR GIFTS**. If you are not serving currently, then pray about where and when God would use you. As Henry Blackaby says in his popular book, *Experiencing God*, look to see where God is working and then join Him.[53]

BE PROACTIVE IN BRINGING OTHERS ON BOARD TO HELP. If our music pastor hadn't asked me to serve, I probably would never have felt competent enough on my own to offer my service. But his faith in me gave me the confidence to move forward and do whatever I could. Remember, you are His workmanship —His masterpiece of art.

God has a plan. In God's plan there are good works prepared before the foundation of the world, just waiting for you. They are designed specifically to be done with **YOUR UNIQUE QUALIFICATIONS**. The Holy Spirit makes Himself clear to each member of the body for the common good of the body. Each and every one of us is gifted by the presence of the Holy Spirit—not for ourselves, but for the benefit of all. Together we can be a healthy and functioning church body.

> Lord, I understand that You use my hands and words to demonstrate Your love for the world. As I surrender all that I am to Your good works, please direct my feet in the way I should go and reveal to me what I am to do and say to others today.

The Wisdom of Age

With the ancient is wisdom;

and in length of days understanding.

—JOB 12:12 (KJV)

I consider myself very fortunate because I knew all my grandparents and my great-grandparents. I was so blessed by their love and wisdom. My paternal grandmother died just a few years ago, and now my own mother is the family matriarch. I love how my nieces and nephews honor her and seek her viewpoint on all sorts of life issues. My oldest nephew adores Grandma. He always makes time in his schedule to spend with her; he calls them "dates" with Grandma. They are both blessed by their time together. This same nephew even seeks my advice in business. I feel so honored that he thinks my opinion is of value.

The Revell Bible Dictionary defines an *elder* as "an ecclesiastical term designating a leader of the faith community."[54] The Hebrew word for elder is *zagen*, which often served in the Old Testament as a political term identifying a leader of tribes, towns or of a nation. While the specific duties of an elder varied over the centuries, the institution itself has been stable right through the New Testament.

Throughout Jewish history the responsibility of the local community rested on predominantly senior citizens who had acquired a reputation for good leadership and wise counsel. This concept of *shared* leadership has a long biblical history that shows how significant the direct participation of the elders was in the life of the community. As members of the community their decisions came not only from knowledge of the Law, but also from an intimate knowledge of the people who made up the community.

Although many things changed within the church during the New Testament times, the church retained this principle of shared leadership by older, respected members of the community. Elders were chosen on the basis of their personal and moral character. The demonstration of growth *through time* allowed them to serve the community as an example of the Christian way of life.

EXPERIENCE IMPARTS A WEALTH OF WISDOM

If this system of shared leadership worked so well for so long, why should it be any different today? One of the problems of society is its fragmentation by ages. We tend to separate ourselves automatically by age, even in our churches. Many older people are finding themselves alone, frustrated and perhaps even disillusioned with the church itself. All the while, these older members are filled with amazing, dynamic potential to guide the younger ones in how to walk in faith, and to counsel them in how to handle life in general, that is, managing home, marriage, family and more. Much of the time, their knowledge is lying dormant, just waiting for an opportunity to express itself.

Perhaps we elders should simply make our own opportunity—to find the time—to share some wisdom instead of *waiting* to be asked. After all, if we have truly gained a bit of knowledge with our years, then certainly we can figure out a way to make use of it. Now that I think about it, there were plenty of times that Grandma or Great-Grandma offered an opinion without my asking for it. Heck, half the time, I was so naïve that I didn't even know there was a question!

The commandment says we are to love the Lord our God with all our hearts and that we shall love our neighbors as we love ourselves. That is a command to get out into the community and get to know our neighbors. After all, community is really all about relationships. First, we are to have an intimate relationship with God, and then loving, healthy relationships with others that build the community. And who said the community has to be limited to the church? As Christians, imagine the difference we could make in this world if we got ourselves involved in more community activities.

Guideposts writer Drue Duke wrote about her own experience regarding elder wisdom:

> The young waitress who was pouring hot coffee for me tarried at the table, talking. She was telling me about the church she attends. She said, "We need more older people in our church for guidance. Their experience and the knowledge they've acquired are priceless to young people."
>
> After she left, I sipped my coffee and pondered her words. I'd never fought growing older, but I never thought of it as being great, either. Now I began to perceive my years as something of a treasure. How many times have I looked back at my youth and thought, *If only I had known then what I know now!*
> But of course such knowledge could not be mine when I

was so young. For then I had not had the failures and disappointments that would prove to me the strength of God's upholding arms. I had experienced neither the deep grief nor the painful heartbreak through which I would learn the never-failing comfort of Jesus Christ. I'd never tasted the bitterness of lonely hours, unbearable except for the presence of the Holy Spirit.

A great satisfaction filled my heart as I realized that the years were a gift from my Lord, not only in their number but in their wealth of wisdom and experience.[55]

Regardless of your age, you have the same wealth of experience within you. Treasure and guard it, build on it and share it. There are many young people—such as those in the waitress's church—who need us and look to us for guidance as they accumulate their years.

When we take the time to look around, we can find plenty of opportunity for sharing all that God has taught us through our lives. We are never too old to learn or too old to teach. If we make the goal a multigenerational experience—where everyone contributes and everyone learns—we can have the best of all worlds.

Just recently, while grocery shopping, I met a wonderful gal in her seventies. She was searching for ways to comply with her doctor's order to consume fewer carbohydrates. She was looking specifically at yogurt. My mom had recently convinced me to try a low-carbohydrate yogurt that she was eating, so I simply gave my new acquaintance the same suggestion. When she thanked me, I told her that it was my mother's idea—not mine. Imagine that—even in my midfifties, Mom is still teaching me to eat right!

SIMPLICITY MADE SIMPLE

Here are ways to make time for sharing the wisdom that experience gives to you:

START WITH THOSE YOU KNOW. If you have grandchildren, then you already have the perfect situation for a mutually beneficial relationship. Grandchildren love their grandparents because grandparents remember what it feels like to be a child. Parents can sometimes make children feel irrelevant, but grandparents can make them feel special. I used to sit at Grandma's feet for hours as she shared her cultural heritage with me. She taught me songs, told me stories and helped build my faith to trust God, especially when things were tough going. I still have a note hanging on my back door that Grandma wrote and tucked inside my suitcase on one of my visits with her. I will cherish it forever.

If you aren't feeling needed, then **FIND A CHILD WITH WHOM TO SHARE YOUR LIFE**. Children have an amazing way of satisfying your longing to feel needed. All they really want is for you to simply spend time with them. It doesn't matter what you do—it's just the fact that you are doing it together. Volunteer at a day care center or start an adopted grandparent group at your church.

BE A MENTOR. My friend Jan was adopted by a wonderful older woman in our community when she first moved here from Colorado. Over the years, she mentored Jan on parenting, housekeeping, hospitality and, most of all, living a life that reflected Christ. Now, as this sweet gal has aged and Alzheimer's is taking its toll, the roles have reversed. But imagine all they would have missed if they had never met. If your church or community doesn't already have a mentor program, then start one. A mentor helps others identify for themselves their strengths and weaknesses and empowers them to continually seek improvement. By using something as simple as asking reflective questions you can help guide your protégée to insightful learning in a nonthreatening way. You might ask, for example, "When your children are grown, what would *you* like to do?" This can be a way of helping them discover ways to begin planning the steps of their new beginning.

GET INVOLVED IN AN INTERGENERATIONAL PROGRAM. More and more communities are supporting the idea of community projects that involve people of all ages. Many are designed to contribute to or benefit the community at large. But the best benefit is the one each generation gains from the exchange with the other. For children, the value and support of a relationship from a nonparent is often that it allows them to openly discuss things they would never discuss with their parents. As a nonparent it is easier for you to have empathy and still be sensitive while encouraging a child to take personal responsibility. Contact your local community service office or city program facilitator to find out what kinds of opportunities are available in your town.

TEACH WHAT YOU KNOW. No matter your age, you still have plenty of time to pass along some wisdom. If you know how to sew, then teach a young girl how to sew doll clothes. (Sewing was one of my favorite pastimes, and I didn't even realize I was learning a skill.) One preschool recently received its accreditation for baking! Yes, after the school explained all that a child can learn from baking cupcakes and cookies, it was awarded the accreditation needed to comply with the state's teaching requirements.

Father, thank You for filling my life with Your wisdom.
Please lead me to someone who needs to hear
my stories of Your faithfulness, to guide them
to what matters most in life. Help me to generously
give what You have freely given to me.

Life Lessons

"Rid yourselves of all the offenses you have committed,

and get a new heart and a new spirit. . . ."

—EZEKIEL 18:31 (NIV)

Life's greatest lessons usually come by learning from our own mistakes. We have all heard the phrase, "If only we could learn from the mistakes of others." But we don't usually learn from others' mistakes. Somehow, some way, we seem to think that we will do things differently, that we won't make the same mistakes as those before us, and then without warning, we do.

Recently, a phone call woke me from a nap and I found myself responding sharply to a person with a not-so-happy tone of voice on the other end. When I hung up, I felt bad. Why did I respond with the same tone of voice that the caller spoke with? That's not like me. But it was me, and that was hard to accept. I am weak. We all have vulnerable times when we simply mess up and offend others.

But God is good. The verse in Ezekiel 18 reminds us that God can change lives and give us a new heart and a new spirit, no matter what may be in our past. His work in us is not something we can do for ourselves. The Holy Spirit does it. If we confess our sins, and turn to God, He will give us a new direction, new love and a new power to change us into what He wants us to be. But change involves our cooperation and our repentance. Sometimes God's new direction requires us to back up a few steps and reflect on where we've been and what we've done in order to proceed forward. It's a little like weeding your garden. You can take the time to do it on a regular basis, or you can wait until it requires a week to work through it. Or, you can let it go even longer and just have it be a weed patch instead of a garden.

Mistakes or wrongs that have been done to us can be weeds in our garden of life. In either case, our time spent living can be so filled with these distracting weeds that we can no longer see what is worthwhile in our lives. These weeds accumulate because we get stuck in time, reminiscing offenses we should have pulled up, let go of and released to God long ago. Instead we seem unwilling or unable to accept the fact that life is hard and we all make mistakes.

TIME OFFERS NEW BEGINNINGS

We need to learn from the past and celebrate the wisdom that experience has granted to us. After all, we now know many ways that didn't work, and we can use those lessons as guidelines for today. If we fill our hearts with the hope of God's promise for abundance and renewal, we will realize that some of life's most painful experiences can become our most valuable, if we let them. The best gift time offers is the ability to start over. I love the way Guideposts writer Madge Harrah expresses it:

When I first started using my word processor, where information is stored on a floppy disk, a writer friend warned me, "If you give a wrong command, you can wipe out a disk, so always keep a backup copy of everything you write."

But I got so confused just learning the basic procedures that I put off learning how to make backups. Then one day I accidentally gave my computer two commands at once and it scrambled forty-seven pages of my novel into garbage. What a shock! For hours afterwards I just wandered around, depressed, discouraged, mad at myself. God had to listen to a lot of prayers that day. It wasn't until the next morning that I found the courage to start over.

Starting over after messing up—boy, is that hard! If it hadn't been for God's support, I don't think I could have done it. But He says over and over in the Bible that He knows we're not perfect and He's standing ready to help whenever we need Him. In fact, no matter *what* we've done, he says that we can, through Him, cast away our transgressions and receive a new heart and a new spirit.

To start over with a new spirit—what a wonderful gift from God![56]

Let's read again what God promises to do: "I will give you a new heart and put a new spirit in you; I will remove from you your heart of stone and give you a heart of flesh. And I will put my Spirit in you and move you to follow my decrees and be careful to keep my laws" (Ezekiel 36:26–27). These verses make it clear that a relationship with God is a partnership that requires us to walk (live) in line with His statutes and keep His commandments. This implies that we still have a choice—to decide to follow His lead or not.

Obviously, I wasn't following His lead when I expressed irritation on the phone with the caller. Without thinking first, I simply didn't make the right choice. That phone call was a reminder to me that to walk this new life, we must daily, and repeatedly, choose how we will spend the precious time we have been given to live. We can be ugly, letting the weeds of offense blind us from seeing the newly seeded garden within us that is waiting to blossom into the best we can be. We simply must allow God to prune the unfruitful vines and pull the weeds so that the new blossoms will live and grow. Or we can rid ourselves of offense, pulling up the weeds that crowd our day, and gaze upon budding sprouts of new life that God has planted to bloom in our future. We alone choose how to use this gift of time.

SIMPLICITY MADE SIMPLE

Here are a few simple ways to enjoy more time in your life:

THINK OF YOUR TIME AS A MEAL, and don't give God leftovers. Which would you rather serve to God, your best meal or leftovers from Tuesday's not-so-hot meatloaf? The same is true of your time. If you are only giving God what little time you have left over at the end of the day or week—it's too little. And it's certainly not your best. God wants and deserves your best.

SPEND TIME IN GOD'S GARDEN. If we are to grow and mature as God expects, then we need to spend time in His garden—His Word. The more time we spend reading and studying His Word, the simpler it will be to remember it and live it.

WEED YOUR LIFE. God wants your whole heart. A life whose soil is filled with weeds is a sign of a preoccupied heart. There are three kinds of weeds that can infest our heart's garden: worries that we attempt to solve without God's help, riches that require more time than they are worth, and pleasures (even good pleasures can become weeds if they cause us to neglect our time with God).[57]

TAKE THE TIME TO FERTILIZE YOUR SOIL. If we are to walk arm and arm with God through the garden of life, then we must be willing to cooperate with what God says. Just as seeds need good soil, so must our hearts be watered with His truth in order that we may receive God's seeds for our lives.

How do you respond to life's challenges? Does your faith seem to wither in times of trouble? Do you question God when needs arise? Then you have to **GET DEEPER ROOTS BY SPENDING MORE TIME WITH GOD**. He knows your trouble and your heart and He wants to give you an abundant life. The key is to be on the alert for opportunities disguised as mistakes. God knows what He is doing—trust Him.

> Lord, I receive the new heart and the new spirit that You willingly have given to me. I will consider wisely how I use the time You have given to me today. I will forgive those who offend me, and I will ask for forgiveness from those I may offend. While I put my trust in You, I know in time I will see Your blessings grow.

Conclusion

A s you close this book, I hope you have learned to live more slowly and more simply. Remember that to have more time and enjoy it more requires us to make choices. Have you discovered a way to drop the unnecessary things from your life? Have you reset your priorities and learned the lesson that quality is more valuable than quantity? I hope so.

A life well lived is one that is lived in balance, in simplicity. Live slowly when you need to. Live fast when it makes sense. Be quick to get your work finished but don't get stuck in the fast lane. Find a speed that makes the most sense for your life—like *tempo giusto* (a musical term for a speed or tempo that fits naturally to the music).

In *Merriam-Webster's Collegiate Dictionary* time is defined as "the measured or measurable period during which an action, process, or condition exists or continues: duration." I find it interesting that the Hebrew Old Testament does not have a general word for an abstract sense of time, nor specific terms for the categories of "past," "present," and "future." Perhaps this is because in Old Testament times they recognized this world simply as a creation of God. As such, it reflects His nature by expressing time in simple, regular and consistent repeated events whose patterns are expressed in days, weeks, months and years.

God has an endless life span and is able to experience all of time—the past, present and future as one. This makes it possible for us to confidently have hope in His perspective of time—eternal. Eternity has no beginning and no end. Like God and His purposes, eternity exists forever. Instead of struggling to fit your lives, your schedules and your dreams into a time frame confined by hours, days, weeks, months and years, take time to catch a glimpse of God's perspective of time for your life. After all, He is in control. We can trust Him to order our weeks and years as we walk through our days. He knows how busy our lives are. All we have to do is start each day by asking Him to order our day. Then we can relax knowing that what didn't get accomplished was not as important to Him as it was to us. And that is what matters most.

Notes

Part One—Facing the Reality of Time

1. Van Varner, in *Daily Guideposts, 1996* (Carmel, New York: Guideposts, 1996), 5.

2. H. D. Thoreau, *Walden* (Ewing, New Jersey: Princeton University Press, 1854), 18.

3. Og Mandino, *University of Success* (New York: Bantam Books, 1982), 213–214.

4. Ibid.

5. Ashton Applewhite, William R. Evans III, Andrew Frothingham, *And I Quote* (New York: St. Martin's Press, 1992), 119.

6. Fulton Oursler, Jr., in *Daily Guideposts, 2002* (Carmel, New York: Guideposts, 2001), 8.

7. Dolphus Weary, in *Daily Guideposts, 1995* (Carmel, New York: Guideposts, 1994), 238.

8. Bruce Feiler, "A Game That Gets Parents and Kids Talking," *Parade* magazine (August 15, 2004), 8–9.

9. Daniel Schantz, in *Daily Guideposts, 1992* (Carmel, New York: Guideposts, 1991), 219.

10. Robert H. Schuller, *You Can Become the Person You Want to Be* (Binghamton, New York: Hawthorn Books, 1998), 20–21.

11. Stephen R. Covey, *The Seven Habits of Highly Effective People* (New York: Fireside, 1989), 149–169.

12. Ibid., 154.

13. Ibid., 153.

14. Hal Urban, *Life's Greatest Lessons* (New York: Fireside, 2003), 128.

15. Denis Waitley, "Life Balance: The Urgent vs. the Important," online article (InspiredGrowth.org, 2002).

Part Two—Using Time Well

16. Eric Fellman, in *Daily Guideposts, 2001* (Carmel, New York: Guideposts, 2000), 146–147.

17. Barbara DeGrate-Sorensen and David Allen Sorensen, *Six Weeks to a Simpler Lifestyle* (Minneapolis, Minnesota: Augsburg Fortress, 1994), 76.

18. See Proverbs 9:11 and James 1:5.

19. Joshua S. Rubinstein et al., "Executive Control of Cognitive Processes in Task Switching," *Journal of Experimental Psychology* (August, 2004).

20. Lee Webber, in *Daily Guideposts, 1992* (Carmel, New York: Guideposts, 1991), 31–32.

21. Infoaging.org, "Stages of Sleep" (September 9, 2004).

22. Fred Bauer, in *Daily Guideposts, 1986* (Carmel, New York: Guideposts, 1985), 149.

Part Three—The Gracefulness of Time

23. Fred Bauer, in *Daily Guideposts, 2000* (Carmel, New York: Guideposts, 1999), 278.

24. *Lancaster New Era* (September 19, 2004).

25. Terry Helwig, in *Daily Guideposts, 1992* (Carmel, New York: Guideposts, 1991), 229.

26. Carol Knapp, in *Daily Guideposts, 1999* (Carmel, New York: Guideposts, 1998), 11.

27. Ulrich Schimmack, *Personality and Social Psychology Bulletin* (August 2004), news release, University of Toronto, WebMD Inc.

28. Jean-Louis Servan-Schreiber, *The Art of Time* (Reading, Massachusetts: Addison-Wesley, 1998), 106.

Part Four—The Time for Change

29. Rob Mullins, Free Speech Online—Blue Ribbon Campaign (www.planetmullins.com 1999).

30. Sue Monk Kidd, adapted from *Guideposts for the Spirit: Stories of Love for Mothers* (2001), 44–48.

31. Don Bell, in *Daily Guideposts, 1988* (Carmel, New York: Guideposts, 1987), 116–117.

32. Gail Sheehy, *New Passages* (New York: Random House, 1995), 180.

33. Ibid., 183.

34. Elizabeth Cody Newenhuyse, *God, I Know You're Here Somewhere* (Minneapolis, Minnesota: Bethany House, 1996), 69.

35. M. Scott Peck, *The Road Less Traveled* (New York: Touchstone Books, 1978), 64.

36. Susan Jeffers, *Embracing Uncertainty* (New York: St. Martin's Griffin, 2003), 94.

37. Jack Horn (www.findarticles.com), in *Psychology Today* (July–August 1989).

38. Dorothy Shellenberger, in *Daily Guideposts, 1992* (Carmel, New York: Guideposts, 1991), 278–279.

39. Newenhuyse, *God, I Know You're Here Somewhere*, 68.

40. Peck, *The Road Less Traveled*, 66.

41. Sue Monk Kidd, in *Daily Guideposts, 1993* (Carmel, New York: Guideposts, 1992), 281–282.

42. Robert J. Wicks, *Everyday Simplicity* (Notre Dame, Indiana: Sorin Books, 2000), 39.

43. Mandino, *University of Success*, 162.

44. Bruce Fisher, EdD, and Robert E. Alberti, PhD, *Rebuilding* (Atascadero, California: Impact Publishers, 2004).

45. Roberta Messner, in *Daily Guideposts, 1999* (Carmel, New York: Guideposts, 1998), 152–153.

Part Five—The Gift of Time

46. Rick Warren, *The Purpose-Driven Life* (Grand Rapids, Michigan: Zondervan, 2002), 20.

47. Isabel Wolseley, in *Daily Guideposts, 1997* (Carmel, New York: Guideposts, 1996), 139–140.

48. Barbara Hughes, *Disciplines of a Godly Woman* (Wheaton, Illinois: Crossway Books, 2001), 58.

49. Psalm 5:3, Psalm 1:2 and Psalm 63:6–7.

50. Jeanne Hill, in *Guideposts* magazine (March 1992), 17.

51. Adapted from Todd Bailey Ministries (www.toddbailey.org/interrupt.htm, 2003).

52. Shirley Pope Waite, in *Daily Guideposts, 1989* (Carmel, New York: Guideposts, 1988), 268–269.

53. Henry Blackaby, *Experiencing God* (Nashville, Tennessee: Broadman & Holman, 1994), 70.

54. Lawrence O. Richards, *The Revell Bible Dictionary* (Grand Rapids, Michigan: Fleming H. Revell, Co., 1990), 332.

55. Drue Duke, in *Daily Guideposts, 1989* (Carmel, New York: Guideposts, 1988), 308–309.

56. Madge Harrah, in *Daily Guideposts, 1986* (Carmel, New York: Guideposts, 1985), 211.

57. Adapted from a sermon by Pastor David Ashcroft, Lancaster County Bible Church: Lancaster, Pennsylvania (October 23, 2004).